Busy Kids™

STORYTIME

Written by:
Jan Brennan
Ann Flagg
Lisa Leonardi
Dayle Timmons

Edited by:
Ada Goren
Kim T. Griswell

Illustrated by:
Susan Hodnett
Rebecca Saunders

Cover designed by:
Kimberly Richard

www.themailbox.com

©1999 by THE EDUCATION CENTER, INC.
All rights reserved.

ISBN #1-56234-241-X

Manufactured in the United States
10 9 8 7 6 5 4 3 2 1

One!

Two!

Busy Kids™
Storytime
Table of Contents

Introduction

Are you tired of searching the library for the perfect stories to round out your favorite thematic units? Then check out the suggested books and literature-based ideas in *Busy Kids™: Storytime*. With recommendations for more than 100 age-appropriate picture books, you'll have a great story to share almost *every* day of the week! And for each selection, you'll find a fresh idea for integrating learning and literature. You can feel confident your little bookworms will love the books and activities because each one was selected with young children in mind.

Tips for Storytime Success:

 Visit your library to gather books for your upcoming themes. Use interlibrary loan to locate books your local library does not have.

 Preread each selected book to become familiar with its characters and plot.

 Be animated! Engage youngsters by reading with drama and enthusiasm. Try using a different voice for each character in a story.

 Pause occasionally while reading to discuss the plot or predict what will happen next.

 Reread favorite books to build on youngsters' love for reading and to develop vocabulary and comprehension skills.

 Put previously read books in your reading center for children to enjoy independently.

 Keep a class reading record by writing titles you've read together on construction paper bookworms that wiggle their way across your classroom walls.

 Introduce *Busy Kids: Storytime* to your school librarian as a resource to use when purchasing books for your school collection.

 Read together *every day!*

BUNNIES AND BASKETS

RABBIT'S GOOD NEWS

Watch your little bunnies' ears perk right up for a reading of *Rabbit's Good News* by Ruth Lercher Bornstein (Clarion Books). The soft and warm pastel illustrations are a natural invitation for your children to make some pastel pictures of their own. To prepare, make several tagboard cutouts of the bunny on page 58. Place the cutouts in your art center, along with markers, white paper, tape, and large sticks of colored chalk in soft colors. Instruct a child to lay a sheet of paper over a bunny cutout; then tape the paper to the table. Have him use the side of a piece of chalk to make a rubbing over the bunny. Encourage him to blend other colors of chalk around the bunny. As a final touch, have him use markers to add facial features. Add a spritz of hairspray to prevent the chalk from rubbing off. It's bunny magic!

LaqUeeta

LITTLE BUNNY'S EASTER SURPRISE

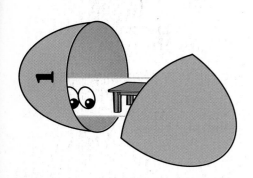

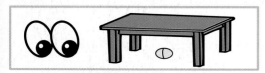

There are all kinds of surprises in store when you read *Little Bunny's Easter Surprise* by Jeanne Modesitt (Simon & Schuster Books for Young Readers). After sharing the story, treat your little ones to a surprise treasure hunt similar to the one in the story. First, create a number of clues (like the one shown) to help your youngsters locate a hidden surprise. Place each clue inside a numbered plastic egg. Set aside egg number one; then put egg number two in the location dictated by the clue in egg number one. Continue to hide the eggs in the appropriate places, so that little ones can follow the clues. Hide a basket of treats—such as a class supply of plastic eggs with jelly beans inside—at the final location.

To begin the hunt, divide your class into the same number of small groups as the number of clues. Give one group egg number one and have group members decipher the clue inside. After the group has searched and found the next egg, have another group follow the directions on the second clue. Continue in this fashion until the last group has discovered the basket. Your little bunnies will be hip-hoppin' with delight to discover their surprise!

THE EASTER EGG ARTISTS

Stress the importance of individuality as you read aloud *The Easter Egg Artists* by Adrienne Adams (Aladdin Paperbacks). Young Orson Abbott was encouraged to develop his own painting style. Do the same for your youngsters by giving them an opportunity to experiment with various painting tools and techniques. Provide new, various-sized paintbrushes as well as other clean painting tools, such as toothbrushes, sponges, cotton swabs, cotton balls, rollers, and feathers. Give each child a small container of water. Invite each child to use the water and painting tools to "water-paint" chalkboards, tabletops, or sidewalks. Encourage him to try making various brush strokes, such as swirls, lines, and zigzags. After ample time for experimentation, give each child a large oval egg cut from tagboard and invite him to use real paints to design an original Easter egg. Compliment each of your young artists on his unique painting style.

THE SPRING RABBIT

When Smudge gets tired of waiting for a brother or sister bunny to arrive, he decides to make his own in *The Spring Rabbit* by Joyce Dunbar (Bantam Books). After reading the story, invite your youngsters to make these unique bunnies from clay and natural materials. First take the class on a nature walk. Invite youngsters to gather twigs, leaves, pine needles, or other small nature items. After returning to the classroom, give each child some clay or play dough. Have the class follow your lead as you mold a portion of clay into a bunny. Roll a small portion of the clay between your hands to form a ball. Roll another larger ball, and then mold them together to form the bunny's head and body. Then shape and attach two long ears to the head. Encourage each child to use his collected nature items to decorate his clay bunny.

THE COUNTRY BUNNY AND THE LITTLE GOLD SHOES

Learn how kindness is rewarded in *The Country Bunny and the Little Gold Shoes* by Du Bose Heyward (Houghton Mifflin Company). After reading this timeless classic (in two sessions for younger listeners), discuss the things that earned Mother Cottontail the golden shoes—her kindness, speed, wisdom, and bravery. Tell youngsters that these qualities deserve to be rewarded, and then show them a small basket. Explain that a jelly bean will be placed in the basket each time a child exhibits one of these qualities. When the basket has a jelly bean for every child, reward the class by making golden shoes like the ones Mother Cottontail received.

Use the pattern on page 58 to cut out a pair of tagboard shoes for each child; then place the cutouts on a newspaper-covered table, along with diluted glue, paintbrushes, gold glitter, yarn, and a hole puncher. Help the child punch a hole in the top of her pair of tagboard shoes. Thread a length of yarn through the hole and tie the ends together to make a necklace. Have the child paint glue onto her tagboard shoes and then sprinkle them with gold glitter. Once they are dry, invite the child to wear the golden shoes around her neck as a reminder of her fine qualities.

Christmas

Elephant and Mouse Get Ready for Christmas

Learn lessons about friendship from a big-hearted friend in *Elephant and Mouse Get Ready for Christmas* by Lois G. Grambling (Barron's Educational Series, Inc.). To prepare for this extension activity, gather and label a large stocking for Mouse and a small stocking for Elephant. Collect a class supply of small toys from your classroom, being sure to include a few toys that are small enough to fit inside the small stocking. As you read the story, pause immediately after Elephant switches the names on the stockings. To help children understand Elephant's act of kindness, lay the stockings on the floor in front of the class and distribute the toys to the children. Ask one child at a time to place his toy inside a stocking. Once all the toys are delivered, ask youngsters to tell you which stocking is holding more gifts. Count to confirm their answer. Ask them to explain why they think Elephant switched the names on the stockings. Encourage predictions about the outcome of this delightful story before you read on.

Only a Star

Programs that celebrate the religious aspect of Christmas will enjoy the story of the first Christmas as told in *Only a Star* by Margery Facklam (William B. Eerdmans Publishing Company, Inc.). Ask youngsters to identify the baby on the cover of the book. Ask student volunteers to describe the story of the first Christmas as they know it. Then read the story to your youngsters, telling them of the star that turns the simplest objects into glistening decorations to welcome baby Jesus. As an extension, invite each child to make a manger scene. Give each child a set

of nativity stickers. (These are available at teacher stores or Christian bookstores. If you can't find them, cut out pictures of Mary, Joseph, and Jesus from used Christmas cards.) To make a manger scene, the child glues four craft sticks in the shape of a manger to a sheet of construction paper. Then he glues (or sticks) the characters inside the manger. Squeeze glue in the shape of a star in the upper corner of the child's nativity scene. Then have him sprinkle gold glitter on top of the wet glue to resemble the magical star from the story.

Counting to Christmas

Capture the Christmas spirit of giving and sharing with a reading of *Counting to Christmas* by Nancy Tafuri (Scholastic Trade Books). As an extension to the story, place a small, artificial Christmas tree in the corner of your classroom. As you lead youngsters in making Christmas crafts, plan a session where youngsters can make two simple ornaments to hang on the tree. Just before winter break, invite parents to a Giving Tree Celebration. Have the children perform holiday songs, and then present each family with the two ornaments their child made for the tree. Suggest that each family keep one ornament for themselves and give the other to a neighbor, relative, or friend. End the celebration with cookies and hot chocolate to go with the warm feelings associated with your Giving Tree.

Christmas Time

Celebrate the merriment of preparing for Christmas through the eyes of a child in *Christmas Time* by Catherine Stock (Aladdin Paperbacks). After reading the story, revisit the illustration of the young girl making Christmas cookies. Then sharpen early scissors skills by inviting your little elves to make Christmas cookies from play dough. Add Christmas cookie cutters and rolling pins to your play dough area. To make a Christmas cookie, a child gently presses the cookie cutter of his choice onto rolled-out play dough to make an imprint. Then he removes the cookie cutter and uses scissors to cut out the shape. Encourage your little bakers to add decorations by pressing colorful beads or rickrack into the play dough cookies. Mmmm! Don't you just love the smell of Christmas cookies?

Where's Prancer?

Oh, dear! Santa has a reindeer missing in *Where's Prancer?* by Syd Hoff (HarperCollins Publishers, Inc.). Use this follow-up activity to sharpen skills with one-to-one correspondence. Make two copies of the reindeer and carrot patterns (page 59). Color the eight reindeer and eight carrots; then cut them out and attach felt to the back of each cutout. As you read the story a second time, pause on the page where Santa discovers that one reindeer is missing. Lay the book aside and use your flannelboard to find out how Santa came to that conclusion. Place seven reindeer on the flannelboard. Give eight children one carrot each, counting them as you distribute each one. Ask one of the eight children at a time to place her carrot next to a different reindeer. Discuss why there is one carrot left over. Then continue reading the story to find out where the missing reindeer has gone. After Prancer's return, repeat the flannelboard activity. Just add the eighth reindeer to the board and redistribute the carrots for a feeding time with a happy ending.

CIRCUS

Ginger Jumps

Your circus audience will be on the edge of their seats rooting for Ginger, the circus dog, in *Ginger Jumps* by Lisa Campbell Ernst (Aladdin Paperbacks). After sharing the story, invite your youngsters to portray circus dogs and practice some gross-motor skills at the same time. First, have each child cut two triangles from brown construction paper. Have her glue the two triangles—dog ears—to a sentence strip headband. Then, with her doggie disguise in place, introduce her to the class, giving her a name that will indicate her circus talent. For example, you might introduce Louis, the Jumping Dog, or Mary Kate, the Skipping Dog. As each of your little ones "bow-wows" the audience, reward her with a treat—such as a cracker or small cookie.

This is Danielle, the Prancing Dog!

LUKE

In the third circus ring, my class saw with me three clowns acting silly.

The Twelve Circus Rings

Clown around with numbers in *The Twelve Circus Rings* by Seymour Chwast (Harcourt Brace & Company). This zany adaptation of "The Twelve Days of Christmas" is sure to motivate little learners to create their own simplified class version. Write the numerals from 1 through 12 in a column on a sheet of chart paper. Then help youngsters brainstorm 12 different circus acts and record them on the list. Ask each child to draw a picture of one of the circus acts listed, being sure to include the matching number of characters in his drawing. (If desired, have children work in pairs to illustrate the larger numbers.) Write text for each drawing; then bind the completed pages together into a class book. As you turn to each new page, sing the words to the Christmas tune, turning back to sing the preceding pages each time.

Star of the Circus

"I'm the star of the circus," claims each circus performer in Michael and Mary Beth Sampson's *Star of the Circus* (Henry Holt and Company), until they all realize that it takes an entire team to put on a circus. To show your youngsters what teamwork is all about, invite them to build a human pyramid. In a large open space, position your class as follows: five children sitting in a row on the floor, four children kneeling behind the first row, three children crouched behind the second row, two children standing behind the third row, and a single child standing on a sturdy chair behind the fourth row. (Adjust the number in each row to suit your class size.) When you begin to build the pyramid, have the first child say, "I'm the star of the circus." As each additional child joins the pyramid, have him say, "No, I'm the star of the circus!" When your pyramid is complete, have the class repeat the story's ending by shouting, "We're all stars of the circus!" Be sure to take a Polaroid® photograph of the pyramid so your little circus stars can admire their daring teamwork.

Barnyard Big Top

When Ben's Uncle Julius brings his circus to the farm, everything goes haywire! Youngsters are sure to go hog-wild over the humor of *Barnyard Big Top* by Jill Kastner (Simon & Schuster Books for Young Readers). Ask your little ones what it would be like if their school were turned into a circus. On a sheet of chart paper, write the sentence "One day a circus came to our school." Invite your youngsters to help you write a class story about the events that might take place. Would the principal walk a tightrope over the playground? Would the lions eat up all the food in the cafeteria? Would the bareback riders give the kids rides to the bus stop? Post the story on a wall and let it keep growing as long as children like. Older students may want to illustrate some of the events. At the end of your unit, reread the final story and encourage youngsters to think of an ending.

Circus

Come one, come all to a big top adventure—captured in Lois Ehlert's *Circus* (HarperCollins Juvenile Books). Prepare this art center activity to help little ones imitate Ehlert's unique graphic art style. For each child, cut several stars and a variety of shapes from fluorescent paper. Stock your art center with the cutouts, black construction paper, scissors, scraps of fluorescent paper, and glue. After sharing the story, ask youngsters to examine Ehlert's illustrations again, noting the shapes used to make the circus characters and the border of stars. Then invite each youngster to visit your art center and arrange some fluorescent shapes on a sheet of black paper to make a circus animal or performer. Invite each artist to glue her design to her paper and then add a border of stars. Display these circus creations on a bulletin board with your own Lois Ehlert–style clown (made from fluorescent poster board shapes) and the title "Circus Shapes."

Community

Hounds Around Town: A Guess-What-They-Do Flap Book

Youngsters will be hounding you to read Megan Halsey's *Hounds Around Town* (Little Simon) over and over again. As you read the story, invite children to lift the flaps to reveal hidden community helpers busy at work. After completing the story, teach the class the following song. Then sing the song together as you browse through the pages of the book. Instead of reading the text again, invite youngsters to name the community helpers they see on each page and give a description of each helper's job. Can they recall who is working behind each flap by looking at the setting for clues? Replace "Houndtown" in the following song with the words "our town," and sing it anytime to review community helpers and their important jobs.

(sung to the tune of "This Old Man")

In Houndtown
All around,
There are helpers to be found.
Let's try to name them one by one.
What are the jobs they must get done?

Who Uses This?

As you study community helpers, hammer home the tools of the trades with a reading of *Who Uses This?* by Margaret Miller (Mulberry Books). After sharing the book, gather pictures of community helpers and collect various tools used by them, such as a police officer's badge, a teacher's chalk, and a chef's mixing bowl and spoon. Display the community helpers with the wrong tool placed in front of each helper. Have youngsters match the correct tool to each community helper and ask them to name other tools that might be used by each one. Later, place the tools in your dramatic-play center and invite your little ones to role-play the duties of each job.

Can I Have a Stegosaurus, Mom? Can I? Please!?

An imaginative little boy asks, *Can I Have a Stegosaurus, Mom? Can I? Please!?* in this tale by Lois G. Grambling (Troll Associates, Inc.). A surprise ending develops as a cracking dinosaur egg hatches and the little boy comes back to his mom with another question: "Can I have a Tyrannosaurus Rex, Mom...Can I? PLEASE!?" Use this ending to spark your youngsters' imaginations about having a prehistoric pet of their own. Invite youngsters to close their eyes and imagine themselves with a giant T-rex. After giving little ones a minute to think, invite each child to complete this sentence: "If I had a T-rex, Mom, I would…" Write down his response on a sheet of paper; then encourage him to illustrate his sentence. Bind the drawings together into a class book. Have youngsters take turns taking this book home to show their moms, who are sure to be delighted that dinosaurs are extinct!

If I had a T-rex, Mom, I would let him sleep in my bed.

My Dinosaur

It's a dream come true in Mark Alan Weatherby's *My Dinosaur* (Scholastic Trade Books) as a little girl has a moonlit adventure with her prehistoric pet. To follow up this dreamy story, make a read-along tape of the story to put in your listening center. Record yourself reading the book in your best dreamy voice. If desired, whistle when the text says the girl whistled; slurp when it says they drank at the river; and sing the goodnight song to the tune of "Happy Birthday to You" (say the last line). At the beginning of the tape, instruct youngsters to turn the page when they hear the sound of a bell (or another chosen signal). Once you're done recording, play the tape for the class as you turn the pages of the book. If necessary, remind youngsters to turn the pages at the sound of the bell. Place the tape and a copy of the book in your listening center for your children to enjoy independently. Sweet dreams!

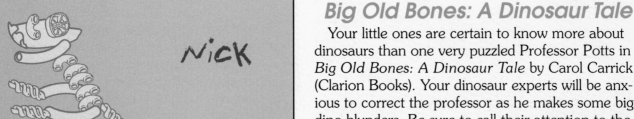

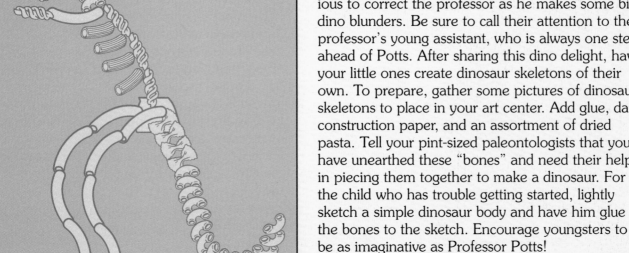

NiCK

Big Old Bones: A Dinosaur Tale

Your little ones are certain to know more about dinosaurs than one very puzzled Professor Potts in *Big Old Bones: A Dinosaur Tale* by Carol Carrick (Clarion Books). Your dinosaur experts will be anxious to correct the professor as he makes some big dino blunders. Be sure to call their attention to the professor's young assistant, who is always one step ahead of Potts. After sharing this dino delight, have your little ones create dinosaur skeletons of their own. To prepare, gather some pictures of dinosaur skeletons to place in your art center. Add glue, dark construction paper, and an assortment of dried pasta. Tell your pint-sized paleontologists that you have unearthed these "bones" and need their help in piecing them together to make a dinosaur. For the child who has trouble getting started, lightly sketch a simple dinosaur body and have him glue the bones to the sketch. Encourage youngsters to be as imaginative as Professor Potts!

The Ugly Duckling

Read aloud Jerry Pinkney's adaptation of *The Ugly Duckling* (Morrow Junior Books) for a thought-provoking lesson in acceptance. (You may want to read the story in two sessions for younger students.) Retold in a sensitive yet dramatic way, this timeless classic will prompt discussion about how our treatment of others can either hurt or heal. As you read the story, pause and ask for comments whenever the duckling is mistreated. Help youngsters verbalize how they think the ugly ducking is feeling and why. After the story, ask your little ones to share examples of times when they have felt excluded or different. In addition, discuss circumstances that have made your youngsters feel good. Divide a sheet of chart paper into two columns, labeled as shown. Brainstorm together a list of words or phrases that fit each category. In the following days, encourage children to use the positive words (or phrases) from your list when interacting with their classmates.

○ Words That Hurt	○ Words That Heal
You can't play.	Want to play with us?
I don't like you anymore.	I like your picture.
You look funny.	I like your dress.
I don't want to be your friend.	Will you be my friend?

The Little Red Hen

Its simple text and cheerful illustrations make Byron Barton's version of *The Little Red Hen* (HarperCollins Children's Books) a fairy-tale delight. Read the story several times to familiarize the children with the characters and plot. As a follow-up, photocopy a class supply of the animals on page 60 onto heavy paper. Give each child a copy. Encourage him to color the animals and then cut them apart. Have him make the animals into puppets by taping them to craft sticks. Provide small paper bags for storing the puppets, and write "Little Red Hen to Go" on the outside of each bag. Reread the story to the class. As each animal is featured, encourage youngsters to hold up the matching puppet. Also encourage youngsters to recite the characters' predictable lines. Continue having students participate in readings until they can use the puppets to tell the tale on their own. Then send the bags home so students can perform it for family and friends.

The Elves and the Shoemaker

Sew a little magic into your day with a reading of *The Elves and the Shoemaker*, retold by Bernadette Watts (North-South Books Inc.). As an extension, invite your little elves to strengthen their fine-motor skills by "sewing" shoes. In advance, trace a shoe onto brown craft foam; then cut out the shoe. Use a hole puncher to make evenly spaced holes around the edge of the foam shoe. Knot one end of a length of black lanyard (or yarn) to one hole in the shoe. (If using yarn, dip the loose end in glue and let it dry.) Make a desired number of shoes in the same manner and place them at a center. Invite your little cobblers to come to the workbench and sew some shoes. Show them how to weave the lacing in and out of each hole in a shoe. They're sure to have fun, right down to the very last stitch!

The Tortoise and the Hare

You'll have little ones on their feet at the conclusion of *The Tortoise and the Hare* as they discover who wins the race between the pokey tortoise and his overconfident opponent. Use this Aesop fable, retold by Janet Stevens (Holiday House, Inc.), to teach youngsters the importance of showing effort even in times of doubt. In advance, make a tortoise pin by hot-gluing half of a walnut shell to a tortoise-shaped background cut from green felt. Glue wiggle eyes to the head. When the glue is dry, hot-glue a safety pin to the back of the tortoise. After reading the story, discuss how Tortoise showed effort even though he didn't think he could win the race. Then seat youngsters in a circle and pass around the tortoise pin. As each child holds the tortoise, encourage her to say, "I was like Tortoise when…" and describe a personal experience when she tried hard and accomplished her goal. Responses might include learning to cut with scissors, ride a bike, or tie shoes. In the following days, pin the tortoise to a child's clothing when she exhibits excellent effort, just as Tortoise did.

The Gingerbread Man

After a reading of Barbara Baumgartner's simple version of *The Gingerbread Man* (Dorling Kindersley Publishing, Inc.), invite little ones to make their own gingerbread men from some spicy-smelling play dough. Mix up a batch of your favorite play dough, adding food coloring to make it brown and two tablespoons of ground ginger to scent it. Give each child in a small group a portion of dough on a square of waxed paper. Encourage the children to roll their dough into snake shapes. Then have them form the snakes into shapes to make the body parts of a gingerbread man, such as a circle for a head, a rectangle for a body, and four ovals to make the arms and legs. If desired, provide raisins and M&M's® candies so little ones can add faces and buttons to their gingerbread creations.

Fall Harvest

Apples and Pumpkins

Enjoy a trip to the farm for some apple and pumpkin pickin' as you read *Apples and Pumpkins* by Anne Rockwell (Aladdin Paperbacks). As a follow-up, invite your youngsters to do some fall harvest estimating. Cut out a class supply of red construction paper apples. Fill a bushel basket (or smaller basket) with real apples. Ask youngsters to guess how many apples are in the basket; then ask each child to record her name and estimation on a construction paper apple. Count the apples together to determine the actual number. Discuss the estimates. Whose was closest? Which were too high? Too low? Then munch and crunch those yummy apples for a snack or use them to make applesauce.

For an "a-peel-ing" bulletin board, tack the empty bushel basket (on its side) to the board and add the paper apples with the children's estimates so that they appear to be spilling out of the basket. Add the poem shown to finish the display.

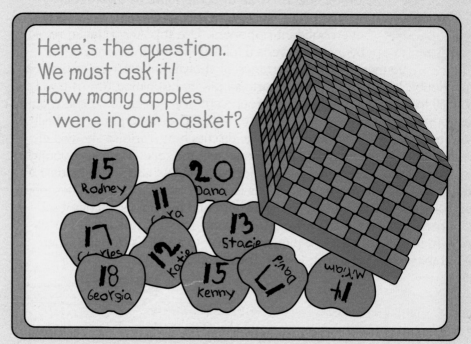

Here's the question. We must ask it! How many apples were in our basket?

15 Rodney • 20 Dana • 11 Cara • 17 Charles • 13 Stacie • 12 Katie • 18 Georgia • 15 Kenny • 17 David • 14 Miriam

Pumpkin Pumpkin

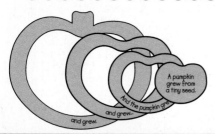

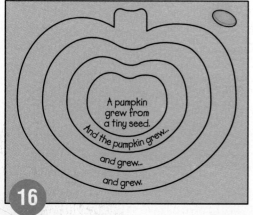

A pumpkin grew from a tiny seed.
And the pumpkin grew...
and grew...
and grew.

You're sure to see youngsters' enthusiasm grow as they watch Jamie's pumpkin grow...and grow...and grow in Jeanne Titherington's *Pumpkin Pumpkin* (Mulberry Books). After sharing this classic, invite your little ones to make pumpkin puzzles. Draw a pumpkin shape (as shown) on orange paper. Program the graduated "rings" on the pumpkin design as shown. Photocopy a class supply of the programmed drawing on orange construction paper. Next, gather a class supply of pumpkin seeds and place them at a classroom center, along with the pumpkin patterns, scissors, and glue.

To make a pumpkin puzzle, the child cuts out the largest pumpkin. Then he folds the cutout in half—with the lines showing on the outside—and cuts out each smaller pumpkin. (Give help as needed.) Once all four pumpkins are cut out, he glues a pumpkin seed to the smallest pumpkin. Show him how to put his pumpkin puzzle together by sequencing the pumpkins from smallest to largest. Help him read aloud the writing on the pumpkin as he assembles it. Store the pumpkin puzzles in resealable plastic bags and encourage children to share them with their families.

Too Many Pumpkins

What's Rebecca Estelle to do when she finds herself surrounded by an entire yard full of pumpkins? Get baking, of course! Read aloud *Too Many Pumpkins* by Linda White (Holiday House, Inc.), then serve up a science lesson as you invite youngsters to observe the differences in raw and cooked pumpkin. Show youngsters a small cooking pumpkin (often called a sugar pumpkin). Have them watch as you use a sharp knife to cut the pumpkin in half crosswise. Cut a small chunk off one half and pass it around for children to examine. Talk about the pumpkin's smell, color, and texture. Then place the pumpkin in a baking pan—cut sides down—and ask an adult helper to bake the pumpkin at 325° for 45 minutes or until tender when pierced with a fork. After it cools, return it to your classroom and have youngsters examine how it has changed. Ask student volunteers to help you remove the peel and seeds. Then have everyone take turns using a potato masher to mash the pumpkin.

If desired, use the mashed pumpkin in place of canned pumpkin in your favorite recipe and bake up a class treat of muffins, bread, or pie. Rebecca Estelle would be proud!

Possum's Harvest Moon

Celebrate along with Possum and his friends as they party under the harvest moon in *Possum's Harvest Moon* (Houghton Mifflin Company). To create a harvest moon in your classroom, put a circle-shaped yellow transparency on the overhead projector and shine it on the ceiling to resemble the moon. Or invite small groups of youngsters to help paint a large circle from bulletin board paper yellow and then sprinkle the wet paint with gold glitter. Hang the finished moon from the ceiling. Once your harvest moon is in place, invite little ones to sing and dance to this moonlight jig.

(sung to the tune of "This Old Man")

The harvest moon
Rose in the sky,
So Possum said, "Let's jump
   and jive.
Come to my Harvest Moon
   Soiree!
We'll sing and dance till the
   break of day!"

Grandma's Smile

Join a young girl and her grandmother as they enjoy the excitement of an autumn fair in *Grandma's Smile* by Elaine Moore (Lothrop, Lee & Shepard Books). What better way to culminate your fall harvest unit than to have your own class fair? Set up these activities that resemble those in the story.

- Ask parent volunteers to send in doughnuts and apple cider for a fall treat.
- Set up pumpkin relays where youngsters roll pumpkins to a designated spot.
- Together rake some leaves into a pile; then jump in them. Or purchase some hay bales and allow little ones to climb on and jump off them.
- Play some festive music and do-si-do like the girl and her grandmother did in the story.
- Set up a few large pumpkins and invite each youngster to use erasable markers to add a jack-o'-lantern face or a face that reminds him of his grandma's smile.

Family

Alligator Baby

When Kristen's parents bring home her new baby brother, it isn't at all what she expected. Read Robert Munsch's hilarious tale *Alligator Baby* (Cartwheel Books); then teach your little ones this song that reviews the story's events. Invite two student volunteers to role-play the parents while the rest of the class pretends to be Kristen. Have the parents stand in front of the class and take turns holding a doll that is completely wrapped in a blanket until the final verse.

(sung to the tune of "He's Got the Whole World in His Hands")

They've got the alligator baby in their hands.
They've got the alligator baby in their hands.
They've got the alligator baby in their hands.
Now take it back to the zoo!   *Shake index finger and put other hand on hip.*

They've got the little seal baby in their hands....
They've got the little monkey baby in their hands....

They've got my little baby brother in their hands.
They've got my little baby brother in their hands.
They've got my little baby brother in their hands.
Now no more zoo for you!   *Shake index finger and put other hand on hip.*

Me and My Family Tree

Joan Sweeney's *Me and My Family Tree* (Crown Publishers, Inc.) provides a simple explanation of how children and their relatives are connected to each other. For a fun follow-up, invite youngsters to make these family treehouses. Set up your art center with a class supply of 4" x 6" house shapes cut from white construction paper; a nine-inch tagboard circle, a 3" x 6" tagboard rectangle, 9" x 12" construction paper in green, brown, and blue; markers; and glue.

A child at this center uses the tagboard patterns to trace and then cut out a green circle and a brown rectangle from construction paper. He forms a tree shape with his cutouts and glues the tree to a blue construction paper background. Next he draws each family member that he lives with on a house shape. He writes (or dictates) the names of his family members under the drawings. Then he glues the house shape to the tree to make a family treehouse.

The Relatives Came

What could be more fun than a summer spent with the relatives? After sharing the joyful fun of Cynthia Rylant's *The Relatives Came* (Aladdin Paperbacks), share these "related" verses to the story.

(sung to the tune of "You Are My Sunshine")

Oh, when the relatives, huggin'-
  kissin' relatives,
Came to visit all summer long,
Oh, there was eatin' and crowded
  sleepin',
When the relatives came along.

Oh, when the relatives, huggin'-
  kissin' relatives,
Came for a visit all summer long,
Oh, there was playin' and music
  makin',
When the relatives came along.

Oh, when the relatives, huggin'-
  kissin' relatives,
Left from their visit all summer long,
Oh, there was dreamin' 'bout the
  very next summer,
When the relatives come back along.

I love you, dear family.
I know you love me, too.
And if I could start over—
Choose a family anew—
You know you can be certain
That I would still choose you!

Horace

Horace by Holly Keller (Mulberry Books) is the tender tale of a little spotted leopard adopted into a family of striped tigers. The story celebrates the ties that bind families together. After reading it, invite youngsters to make these heart-shaped love poems for their families. First, copy the poem shown and duplicate it for each child. Make heart-shaped patterns from tagboard and place them at your art center along with the poem copies, construction paper, colorful curling ribbon, hole punchers, scissors, and tape.

To make a love poem, trace a heart pattern onto construction paper, cut it out, and then glue the poem to the heart. Punch holes around the outside of the heart. Tape one end of a length of curling ribbon to the back of the heart, and then lace the ribbon through the holes. Secure the ribbon by taping the loose end to the back side. Have each child take his love poem home to his one-of-a-kind family.

One Hundred Is a Family

Pam Muñoz Ryan embraces many different types of families—both traditional and nontraditional—in *One Hundred Is a Family* (Hyperion Press Limited). After sharing this cheerful counting book with your class, discuss how your classroom is a family connected by bonds of friendship. Then cut out a large schoolhouse shape from red bulletin board paper and mount it on a bulletin board. Give each child a sheet of white drawing paper and markers, and encourage her to draw a full-length picture of herself. Have her cut around her drawing and glue her picture to the schoolhouse. Invite any adults who work with your class to draw self-portraits, too. Once the pictures are glued to the schoolhouse, count together all the people in your class family and insert the number into the title "[Number] is a family sharing a classroom."

The Farm

I Went Walking

You'll be surprised at whom you bump into as you stroll along with the young child in Sue Williams's *I Went Walking* (Harcourt Brace & Company). Have youngsters look for a clue in each illustration to help them predict which farm animal will appear on the following page. As a fun follow-up, cut a small square from a sheet of construction paper. Out of sight of the children, place a toy farm animal or a farm animal picture behind the opening in the paper so that only a portion of the animal shows. Encourage a student volunteer to say, "I went walking." Have the class respond, "What did you see?" Then have the volunteer guess the hidden farm animal and say, "I saw a [name of farm animal] looking at me." Remove the construction paper to reveal the hidden animal. Continue in this manner, reciting the text and guessing other hidden farm animals.

This Is the Farmer

Give your youngsters a taste of farm life by reading *This Is the Farmer* by Nancy Tafuri (Greenwillow Books). Set up a milking station to show your farmhands what it is like to milk a cow like the farmer does in the story. Place a bucket on top of newspaper or a towel. Fill a latex glove with water, and then wrap an elastic band around the opening of the glove. Use a straight pin to prick holes in the four fingertips (excluding the thumb). Next use a permanent marker to draw a cat face on a plastic plate to represent the cat that gets a squirt of milk on the last page of the story. Tape the cat to the wall (next to the bucket) and cover the area below it with old towels or newspaper.

To use the milking station, one child holds the glove over the bucket, allowing the "teats" to dangle. Another child wraps four fingers around one "teat," with her thumb at the top. She firmly presses her thumb and index finger together to create pressure, and then slowly moves her fingers down until she squirts "milk" into the bucket. Once she has learned to "milk," have her try to aim a squirt of "milk" at the cat.

Going to Sleep on the Farm

A little boy asks, "How does a cow go to sleep?" and his father answers in *Going to Sleep on the Farm* by Wendy Cheyette Lewison (Puffin Books). This beautifully illustrated book has patterned and predictable text that your youngsters will soon catch on to. To help them enjoy the book further, make a classroom tape that will become a down-home favorite in your listening center. To prepare, read the book aloud several times, inviting the class to join in to provide the animal sounds and the "Shhh" sound at the end. After a few rehearsals, pop a blank tape into your tape recorder and read the book again with your students' help. Place the completed tape and a copy of the book in your listening center for all to enjoy.

Big Red Barn

Round up your little farmhands for a reading of *Big Red Barn* by Margaret Wise Brown (HarperCollins Publishers, Inc.). Call attention to the baby farm animals and their parents. Then follow up with your own simplified version of this barnyard tale. To prepare, program a sheet of copy paper with the text shown, leaving the blanks unprogrammed. Next, draw a simple barn shape (approximately 9" x 5") on another sheet of copy paper. For each child, photocopy the programmed page onto copy paper and the barn onto red construction paper. Cut out each barn and then make a T-shaped cut as shown. Glue the top and sides of each barn to a separate programmed sheet, above the text. Invite a child to fold open the barn doors and draw a mother farm animal and her baby inside the barn. Help him complete the sentence about his farm animals. Bind the completed pages into a class book titled "Our Big Red Barn."

In the big red barn there was a big _pig_ and a little _pig_.

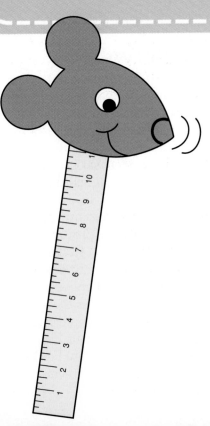

Cock-a-doodle-doo: A Farmyard Counting Book

You'll reap a harvest of learning when you read *Cock-a-doodle-doo: A Farmyard Counting Book* by Steve Lavis (Lodestar Books). In advance, use the story text to create a read-along chart. Write "1 One noisy rooster" on the first line of a sheet of chart paper. Continue recording the lines of text in this manner until you have recorded all ten animals. Then cut a mouse head shape from brown craft foam to resemble the mouse in the story. Glue a wiggle eye on the mouse; then tape him onto the tip of a ruler to make a pointer. Reread the story, inviting a student volunteer to use the mouse pointer to point to the mouse on each page. Next, read the chart together as one student volunteer runs the mouse pointer under the words. Have another volunteer turn the corresponding pages of the book. On subsequent days, count on this chart to help you reinforce numerals, number words, or initial consonant sounds.

The Five Senses

My Five Senses

Five young children take the reader on a photographic tour of the senses in *My Five Senses* by Margaret Miller (Aladdin Paperbacks). After reading through the book once, turn to the introduction page that features pictures of each of the five children pointing to body parts that go with their senses. Point to the first child's picture and say, "Eyes are for...," inviting the class to complete the sentence with the word *seeing*. Repeat this for each of the five pictures, focusing on the featured body part. Next, open the book to any two-page spread. Ask the children to name the sense that is being used in each photograph. If a clue is needed, provide the corresponding body part. It's a follow-up activity that just makes sense!

Hands are for touching !

Charles

The Story of Ferdinand

The Story of Ferdinand by Munro Leaf (Viking Press) was first published more than 50 years ago and has stood the test of time as generations have enjoyed the simple story of the peaceful bull that would rather smell flowers than fight. After sharing this story with your little ones, set up a smelling center with drawing paper and a combination of scented and unscented markers. Invite individual children to sort the markers into two groups: scented and unscented. If possible, provide two matching sets of scented markers so students can also pair together markers with the same scent. After the child has finished sorting, encourage him to sniff the scented markers and guess the scent of each one. (Be prepared for some colored noses after this activity!) Then encourage your Ferdinand fans to use the scented markers to draw Ferdinand sitting "just quietly" and smelling the flowers.

Popcorn smells ___buttery___.
Popcorn tastes ___salty___.
Popcorn feels ___crunchy___.
Popcorn looks ___white___.
Popcorn sounds ___fast___.

My Five Senses

Aliki's *My Five Senses* (Harper Trophy) helps youngsters understand how we experience things with the help of our senses. After reading the simple text, teach your children the following song to reinforce their knowledge of the senses and their corresponding body parts.

(sung to the tune of "Do You Know the Muffin Man?")

Do you know how I [see] things?
How I [see] things? How I [see] things?
Do you know how I [see] things?
I [see] things with my [eyes].
Point to the body part.

Sing additional verses for the other senses.

You Smell and Taste and Feel and See and Hear

Experience a dog day afternoon through the senses of a delightful dog in *You Smell and Taste and Feel and See and Hear* by Mary Murphy (DK Publishing, Inc.). Then try this extension that will put little ones' five senses to work. Put a bag of microwave popcorn in the microwave (or pour kernels into a hot air popper) without the children seeing. Invite them to close their eyes and listen. As they hear and smell the popcorn popping, have them name the body parts and senses they are using. Can they tell you what is happening? When the popcorn is done popping, show it to the class and invite each child to put a handful of popcorn on a napkin. How does the popcorn look and feel? Now have them enjoy the taste. Next write the phrases shown on your chalkboard and encourage the class to provide the endings.

Another "Sense-ational" Idea

Select any page from *You Smell and Taste and Feel and See and Hear* or a page that features a sensory experience from either of the two *My Five Senses* books and discuss the sense or senses being used in the picture. Then give each child a copy of the reproducible on page 61. Encourage the child to draw a smiley face in each column that shows a sense being used in the illustration. Continue in this manner using other pages from these five-star five-senses books.

Friends

One of Each

Oliver Tolliver learns a valuable lesson about sharing in *One of Each* by Mary Ann Hoberman (Little, Brown and Company). As a follow-up, help your youngsters practice sharing just as Oliver does in the story. Divide your class into pairs; then give each set of friends a banana, a napkin, a pair of scissors, and a plastic knife. Have the class repeat this line from the story, "Why one, simply one, only one, one of each?" Then challenge the friends to figure out a way to enjoy the fruit together. If necessary, direct them to use their scissors to cut the napkin in two and then use their knife to cut the fruit in two. Then remind them of Oliver's words of wisdom: "Eating with friends was the best thing of all. "

To you, my friend,
My hand I give.
We are best friends,
Wherever we live.
Glenda

We Are Best Friends

Read aloud *We Are Best Friends* by Aliki (William Morrow & Company, Inc.) to show youngsters that best friends can remain close even if one has to move away. Invite youngsters who have been separated from a friend to discuss how it made them feel. Then reinforce the idea that best friends can be friends forever by making these special friendship cards. In advance, copy the poem shown and duplicate it for each child. Trim off the excess paper around each copy. Provide youngsters with 9" x 12" construction paper, crayons, and scissors. Have each child fold his paper in half and then place one hand on the paper with his wrist on the fold. Help him trace around his hand; then have him cut around the outline through both thicknesses of paper to create a card made in the shape of his hand. Encourage him to decorate the card's cover and glue the poem to the inside of the card. After he signs his name, send the card home in an envelope to be addressed and sent to a dear friend. Note: *Best Friends Together Again* by Aliki (Greenwillow) is an uplifting sequel to this book.

Mouse	Mole	Otter	Raccoon
neat	messy	too wild	laughs when Cat falls down
likes same games			

George and Martha

Capture the true meaning of friendship by reading this series of stories about the world's two best friends, *George and Martha* by James Marshall (Houghton Mifflin Company). There are many lessons to be learned from these two "hip" friends, so be sure to discuss with youngsters how to apply these lessons in their own friendships. Then follow up with the following song that celebrates friendship.

(sung to the tune of "London Bridge")

[George and Martha] are great friends,
Are great friends, are great friends.
[George and Martha] are great friends.
Hooray for friendship!

Insert the names of other famous friends into the poem, such as Arthur and Buster, Pooh and Piglet, or Mickey and Goofy. Or insert the names of friends from your very own classroom.

Wanted: Best Friend

In *Wanted: Best Friend* by A. M. Monson (Dial Books for Young Readers), Mouse is just the right kind of best friend for Cat. After reading aloud this comical story about friendship, ask youngsters to describe the characteristics of a best friend. Discuss how Cat learns the hard way that true friendship involves some give-and-take. Then divide a sheet of chart paper into four columns. At the top of the first column, write "Mouse." Then list together the reasons why Mouse is the right kind of best friend for Cat. For example, he is neat, unselfish, respectful, and forgiving, and he shares the same interests with Cat. At the top of the remaining columns, write the names of the other animals that want to be Cat's best friend; then list why each animal is not the right kind of best friend for Cat. Your youngsters are sure to learn from Cat that a true best friend is someone to treasure.

My Best Friend

My Best Friend by Pat Hutchins (Greenwillow Books) will help youngsters learn that best friends have their own special gifts to offer one another. After reading the book, discuss how each character has her own unique strengths that make her a good friend. Then give your little ones the opportunity to share their strengths with a friend. Pair each child with a friend. Then encourage each child in a pair of friends to show what she can do well in the classroom, such as build with blocks, complete a puzzle, or draw. When each child has shared her talents with her partner, invite all the children to form one large circle. Ask each child to complete the following sentence: "My friend, [child's name], is really good at _____." That's exactly what good friends do well—make one another feel great!

My friend Nick is really good at singing songs.

Garden

Sunflower House

One child's active imagination turns an ordinary sunflower garden into a sunflower house and more in Eve Bunting's *Sunflower House* (Voyager Picture Books). For a flowery follow-up, invite your little seedlings to grow into beautiful sunflowers with the help of this action rhyme. Seat the children in a circle; then set a plastic sandwich bag with a few sunflower seeds in front of each child. Encourage youngsters to follow along as you lead them in the suggested motions.

Pull up the weeds.
Sow all the seeds.
Water them every day.

Make pulling motion with hands.
Take one seed from bag and pretend to plant.
Pretend to hold a garden hose.

Stems grow fast.
Flowers here at last!
A sunflower house! Hooray!

Crouch; then stand tall.
Put hands together overhead.
Lean toward center of circle with hands overhead.

At summer's end,
Flowers start to bend,
So, I store their seeds away!

Bend at waist; pour seeds out of bag onto floor.
Sit and collect seeds in bag.

Dandelion Adventures

What happens when the wind sends tiny dandelion seeds flying into the air? Read aloud *Dandelion Adventures* by L. Patricia Kite (The Millbrook Press, Inc.) to find out. After reading the story, invite youngsters to make their own dandelions from clay. To prepare, cut enough cotton swabs in half so that each child will have seven. Give each child his seven cotton-swab halves, a small ball of clay, and a craft stick. To make a dandelion, the child pushes his craft-stick stem into the clay. Then he gently inserts the cut ends of the swabs around the perimeter of the clay ball. As you re-read the story, invite youngsters to use their dandelions to practice simple subtraction. As each seed parachute flies and lands somewhere, have each youngster make one swab fly away and land in front of him. Then have the child count to see how many seed parachutes are left on the dandelion. Be sure to help youngsters compare their subtraction with the dandelion picture provided at the bottom of each page. Have youngsters continue in this manner until all seven seed parachutes have landed. If desired, collect all the dandelion seed parachutes and have older children count them to see how many dandelion seeds were dispersed altogether. Now *that's* some dandy math practice!

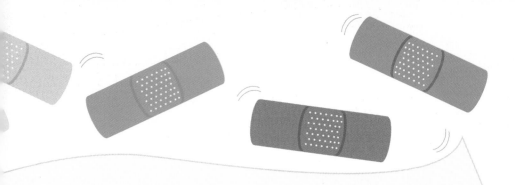

Dr. Kanner, Dentist With a Smile

Come along on a visit to a friendly dentist when you read *Dr. Kanner, Dentist With a Smile* (Children's Press) by Alice K. Flanagan. This story makes a wonderful introduction to a visit from a local dentist or dental hygienist. Explain to your students—just as Dr. Kanner does in the book—that your visitor also works hard to help people keep their teeth and gums healthy. Ask your visiting dental professional to show your youngsters the proper technique for tooth brushing. And after the visit, invite youngsters to make a special thank-you note for your visitor. Cut a sheet of white poster board into a large tooth shape. Program the cutout with a message similar to the one shown, and then invite all your little ones to sign it.

> We don't want to brag, to boast, or to gush. But our teeth look GREAT since you showed us how to brush!
> Thanks from Mrs. Flagg's class
> Mary Joe Sam Teena

Red, Yellow, Green...What Do Signs Mean?

Your youngsters are sure to show signs of interest as you read Joan Holub's *Red, Yellow, Green...What Do Signs Mean?* (Cartwheel Books). Before reading the story, place a small sticky note over each sign in the book. Distribute evenly the sign stickers provided in the book. As you read the story, ask each youngster to hold up his sticker when he sees or hears clues related to his sign in the text. If necessary, peel off the sticky note and have youngsters look at the sign sketch to find the matching sticker. As a fun extension of this story, take the children outdoors for a sign search. Walk through your school's or center's neighborhood looking for different kinds of signs, such as a stop sign, a school crossing sign, or a speed limit sign. Discuss the meaning of each sign you see.

Officer Buckle and Gloria

Your little ones will be barking for more as you culminate your health and safety unit with a reading of Peggy Rathmann's *Officer Buckle and Gloria* (The Putnam Publishing Group). After reading the book, read the safety tips provided inside the front and back covers of the book. Ask youngsters to review the tips they have learned from the book and from your study of health and safety. Write each tip mentioned on a construction paper star. Then divide your class into pairs and give each pair a star. Read the tip to the pair without the rest of the class listening. Then assign one child in each pair to play the part of Officer Buckle, and have the other child role-play Gloria. Direct "Gloria" to first demonstrate the tip on their star, and then have "Officer Buckle" recite the tip. Allow each pair time to practice before they perform their safety tip for the class. If desired, invite them to use props.

When it's time for the safety speech, challenge the class to guess the safety tip performed by each "Gloria" before "Officer Buckle" recites it. Later, post the tips around your classroom as star-studded safety reminders.

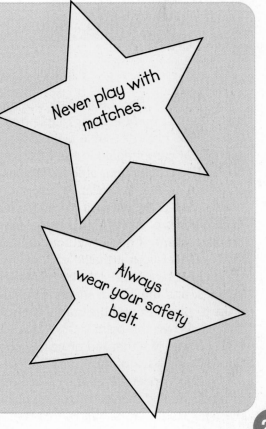

Never play with matches.

Always wear your safety belt.

Leaves

Oakley's Storytime

Take on the role of Oakley the mighty oak tree when you share books about leaves with your little leaf lovers. Introduce yourself (in your deepest voice) as an oak tree who loves to read books to children about your favorite topic—leaves! Pretend to be Oakley each time you share one of the stories in this unit. To create a treelike appearance, hot-glue real or silk leaves to an old pair of gloves to wear on your hands. Make a leaf hat to wear by hot-gluing leaves to a sentence strip and then stapling the ends of the strip together to fit your head. Your youngsters' enthusiasm over Oakley's storytime will make it worth going out on a limb for!

Red Leaf, Yellow Leaf

Lois Ehlert's *Red Leaf, Yellow Leaf* (Harcourt Brace Jovanovich, Publishers) uses colorful collages to trace the history of a sugar maple tree. After sharing this simple story, return to the first page of the book to examine Ehlert's maple leaf cutout. Flip the page back and forth to see the clever effect. Look for the maple leaf cutout again in the final pages of the book. Then invite your little illustrators to create a leaf cutout that is similar to Ehlert's.

For each child, cut a single maple leaf shape from a sheet of white construction paper. (Vary the placement of the leaf cutout on each child's sheet.) Cover your art table with newspaper; then set it up with autumn-colored paints, paintbrushes, and the cutout sheets. Encourage each artist to paint around the cutout on his sheet as desired. When the paint is dry, have each child tape a sheet of either red or yellow construction paper to the back of his painted paper so that his maple leaf appears to be the color in the background. Display these colorful fall paintings with the title "Red Leaves, Yellow Leaves."

Mitchell

I Eat Leaves

"Unbe-leaf-able" as it may sound, we do eat leaves! JoAnn Vandine's *I Eat Leaves* (Mondo Publishing) explains that—just like many animals—we also eat leaves. Caution your youngsters that they are not to eat just *any* leaf from a plant or tree. Then see if they can name some edible leaves, such as lettuce, cabbage, or turnip greens. After your discussion, teach your little ones this song about leaf eaters.

(sung to the tune of "The Farmer in the Dell")

[Koalas] munch on leaves.
[Koalas] munch on leaves.
While they lunch, they munch and crunch.
[Koalas] munch on leaves.

Create additional verses by substituting these other leaf eaters from Vandine's book for the underlined word: *pandas, caterpillars, rabbits, giraffes, children.*

Fall Is Not Easy

Fall Is Not Easy by Marty Kelley (Zino Press Children's Books) is a humorous look at a tree's many attempts to change its colors with the changing season. After sharing this rhyming text, encourage your little ones to join you at the art table to make silly trees of their own. Set up the center with white construction paper, pencils, several corks, paintbrushes, and tempera paint in different colors. Show the children how to draw a simple tree outline with a pencil or draw the tree shape yourself for younger students. Then en-

courage children to use their imaginations to decorate their trees in a unique way. Younger children may simply want to dab a cork into the autumn colors and make prints on their trees. Older children may paint their treetops like a rainbow, a smiley face, or a hamburger as Kelley does in his story, or they may create their own unique leaf designs.

Autumn Leaves

Explore shapes and colors with Ken Robbins as he teaches youngsters about 13 different trees and the changes that occur in them during the season of autumn. After reading Robbins' *Autumn Leaves* (Scholastic Inc.), invite the class to search your schoolyard for colorful fall foliage. Try to match the leaves with Robbins's photographs from the book. Then further explore the look of fall leaves with a leaf-making station. To prepare, cover your art table and surrounding floor with newspaper; then place a large bowl of water on the newspaper-covered floor. Die-cut three to

five leaves for each child from colorful construction paper. Pour water-thinned paint in fall colors into separate Styrofoam® trays. Clip a piece of sponge to each of several spring-type clothespins; then put a few clothespin paintbrushes in each tray of paint. Have youngsters wear smocks at this station.

To make an autumn leaf, a child uses one hand to crumple a construction paper leaf of his choice; then he opens it and flattens it with his hand. (Younger children may need help with this step.) Using the clothespin paintbrushes, he dabs his leaf with paints in different colors. Next, he swishes his leaf in the bowl of water to blend the colors. Then he places the leaf on newspaper to dry. Use these beautiful, real-istic-looking leaves as an autumn bulletin board border or encourage each child to glue his dried leaves to a black construction paper background for a dramatic display.

Nursery Rhymes

Mary Had a Little Lamb

Share Bruce McMillan's charming photo-illustrated version of the classic *Mary Had a Little Lamb* by Sarah Josepha Hale (Scholastic Trade Books). Then invite each of your little animal lovers to describe a real or imaginary pet of his own. At the bottom of a sheet of paper, insert the child's name and pet into a sentence similar to the one shown. Have the child draw a picture of himself with his favorite animal friend above the sentence. (You might have younger children use magazine pictures of animals.) Invite each child to share his picture with the class as you read the text for this simple nursery rhyme adaptation.

[Wesley] had a [big elephant].
They loved each other so.
And everywhere that [Wesley] went
The [elephant] was sure to go.

After sharing each child's version of the nursery rhyme, bind the pages together for a class book that is sure to make your children laugh and play!

Wesley had a big elephant.

Big Fat Hen

"One, two, buckle my shoe." Come count to ten with the big fat hen and a coop full of chicks in Keith Baker's *Big Fat Hen* (Voyager Picture Books). Then pluck some feathers (from a craft-supply store) for this art activity. Set up your art center with paper, feathers, and a muffin tin of paints in varied colors. Encourage a child at this center to use a feather as a paintbrush to paint his entire paper. (Afterward, wash the feathers to be used again.) Once the paint dries, die-cut numerals from the feather paintings. (Or have older children use stencils to trace the numerals onto their feather paintings and then cut them out.) Reread the story slowly. As you say each number, encourage the children to hold up the matching numeral(s) that they have made. "Nine, ten, let's do it again!"

One!

Two!

To Market, to Market

Anna Miranda's hilarious twist to the familiar nursery rhyme *To Market, to Market* (Harcourt Brace) is sure to make your little ones laugh out loud! After reading the story, invite the class to make cabbage soup using ingredients from the story.

Cabbage Soup

1 baking potato
2 individual stalks of celery
1 beet (or small can of sliced beets)
2 large tomatoes
a handful of pea pods
  (or frozen snow pea pods)
1 bell pepper

1 garlic clove
half a cabbage
1 cup brown rice
4–6 carrots
1 onion
a handful of fresh or frozen okra
salt
pepper

Precut the vegetables into strips. Invite the children to use plastic knives to chop the potato, celery, beet, bell pepper, carrots, and okra into bite-size pieces. Chop the tomato, onion, and cabbage. Encourage the children to taste any vegetables that are new to them. Add the rice, garlic, and pea pods; then cover with water. Add salt and pepper to taste. Cook this hearty cabbage soup on medium heat until the potatoes and carrots are soft. "Yummity Yum!"

Hey Diddle Diddle & Other Mother Goose Rhymes

Add a little music to the rhythm and rhyme of Tomie dePaola's *Hey Diddle Diddle & Other Mother Goose Rhymes* (Paper Star). Choose rhymes from dePaola's collection that have a tune, such as "Baa, Baa, Black Sheep," "Hickory Dickory Dock," and "Rub-a-dub-dub." Use a kazoo to hum the tune before reading the rhyme. Can your youngsters guess the rhyme just by the tune? Give your little musicians some instruments, such as rhythm sticks and sand blocks. Distribute the different instruments evenly among your class. As you share one of the rhymes, encourage your little ones to play along while keeping the steady beat of the rhyme. Alternate instruments between verses or lines. Mother Goose has never sounded so good!

Little Lumpty

Your little ones will really crack up as you share the humor and whimsy of *Little Lumpty* by Miko Imai (Candlewick Press). As an "eggs-tension," set up Humpty's wall for those who are eager to experience it as Little Lumpty did. Place a row of cardboard blocks flat on the floor. (Or put a length of tape on the floor.) Invite a child to sit on the "wall" as you insert her name into the rhyme below. After chanting the rhyme together, listen to the giggles as the child pretends to fall from the wall just like Humpty and Lumpty.

[Courtney] Dumpty [sat] on the wall.
[Courtney] Dumpty had a great fall!

As a variation, try substituting other action words for *sat,* such as *walked, tiptoed, danced,* or *slept.*

Nutrition

Bread and Jam for Frances

Frances the badger learns an important lesson about eating in Russell Hoban's *Bread and Jam for Frances* (Harper Trophy). Before introducing the book to your class, divide a sheet of chart paper into two columns. Label the columns as shown. Hold up the book and introduce Frances. Ask youngsters what Frances is holding in her hands (bread and jam). Then give each child a taste of jam on a cracker. Have each child decide whether or not he likes the taste of jam, then write his name in the appropriate column on the chart. Then read the story to find out how Frances feels about jam. Discuss the story's ending and explain to your little ones that trying new foods can be a step towards healthful eating. And, after all, variety is the spice of life!

I like jam.	I don't like jam.
Marilee	Kyla
Kent	Desireé
Arthur	
T. J.	
Alexis	
David	

Another Bite of Bread and Jam

If reading *Bread and Jam for Frances* leaves your youngsters hungry for jam, gather your little chefs in a circle and follow these simple directions for making your own jam.

Jam in a Bag

2 cups clean, capped strawberries (or raspberries)
2 cups sugar
1 tablespoon lemon juice
1/4 of a 6-oz. package of liquid fruit pectin

Slice the berries in half and place them in a large resealable plastic bag. Then put them inside another bag and seal both bags shut. Pass the bag around your circle and have each child squeeze the bag until the berries are crushed. Measure one cup of crushed berries into a third resealable bag, add the sugar, and let the mixture stand for ten minutes. (Discard the remaining crushed berries.) Combine the pectin and lemon juice; then add it to the berries. Double-bag the berries and seal the bags closed. Pass and squeeze the bag for three minutes or more. (If desired, pass the time by chanting the rhyme that Frances sang about jam.) Next, ladle the jam into a jar (or another container). Let it stand at room temperature for two hours or until the jam is set. Serve the finished jam on bread, just the way Frances likes it! If desired, spread your school-made jam on one half of each child's bread and store-bought jam (of the same flavor) on the other half. Take a vote to see which jam your little ones like better, and chart the results. Store any leftovers in the refrigerator for up to three weeks.

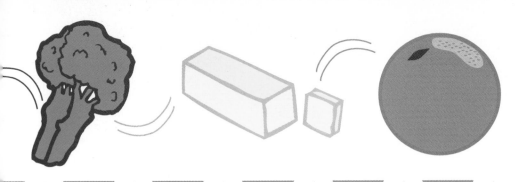

Eating the Alphabet: Fruits and Vegetables From A to Z

From apples to zucchini, teach youngsters about healthful foods with some help from Lois Ehlert's *Eating the Alphabet* (Harcourt Brace & Company). In advance, ask each child to bring a canned fruit or vegetable from home. Lay a set of letters on the floor in alphabetical order. As you read Ehlert's alphabet book a second time, pause after each letter to help children place the canned foods beginning with that letter near it on the floor. By the end of the story you will have your own version of fruits and vegetables from *A* to *Z*.

For further sorting practice, place the canned goods in a classroom center for youngsters to sort by type or brand. Or have individual students sort the cans into these two groups: "Foods I like" and "Foods I don't like." Remind youngsters that they should eat five fruits and vegetables a day, so encourage them to select at least five canned foods they like. When your class is finished with the cans, donate the food to a local food bank or homeless shelter to encourage healthful eating for all.

Gregory, the Terrible Eater

Gregory is not your average goat. He wants fruits and vegetables instead of "normal" goat food, such as cans and coats. Youngsters will giggle when you read about this picky eater's journey to a well-balanced goat diet in *Gregory, the Terrible Eater* by Mitchell Sharmat (Scholastic Trade Books). Follow up the story by inviting youngsters to make open-faced sandwiches for Gregory. In advance, collect small junk items that can be glued to paper, such as small plastic lids, paper clips, bottle caps, scraps of paper and cloth, pencil stubs, and old buttons. Cut a class supply of bread slices from brown or white construction paper. To make a goat sandwich, a child glues her paper bread slice to a paper plate. Then she glues a variety of junk to the bread. Ask the child to give her sandwich a name, such as "A Paper Clip and Button Sandwich on Wheat." Write the title on a strip of paper and post the sandwich and its title on a bulletin board titled "Goat Sandwiches for Gregory."

A Paper Clip and Button Sandwich on Wheat

Lunch

The little mouse in Denise Fleming's *Lunch* (Henry Holt and Company) certainly is a healthy eater! He likes fruits and vegetables in all colors of the rainbow. After sharing this story with your youngsters, invite them to make these simple, colorful booklets that reflect their own food choices. To prepare, program a sheet of copy paper with this sentence: I eat _____. Photocopy four or five of these pages for each child. Then invite youngsters to thumb through magazines or seed catalogs to find pictures of fruits and vegetables they like to eat, making sure that each food they select is a different color. Have each child cut out and then glue a picture to each of her pages. Then write or dictate the color and food to fill in the blank. Once all her pages are completed, bind them together between covers and title her book "[Child's name]'s Rainbow of Good Foods."

I eat green beans.

Ocean

That's a star!

At the Beach

Get your little bathing beauties ready for a trip to the beach. Before reading *At the Beach* by Anne and Harlow Rockwell (Aladdin Paperbacks), pack a beach bag with items you might take to the beach, such as sunglasses, sunscreen, a pail, a shovel, a towel, a book, a juice box, and a bag of pretzels. Make sure you have one item in the bag for each child. After enjoying the story together, tell the class you are going on an imaginary trip to the beach. Pass the beach bag around your group as they sit in a circle, and have each child select one item to hold. Next recite the following poem:

Let's go to the beach.
Let's pack up right away.
Let's bring everything we need
For the perfect beach day.

Now give a child the empty beach bag and have her say, "I will pack [item]." She then places her object in the bag and passes it to the next child. That child says, "I will pack [the previous item] and [his item]," as he puts his item in the bag. Continue in this manner until every child has had a turn. Encourage youngsters to name the items in the same order as they were placed in the bag. If a child has difficulty remembering the items, solicit help from the class.

I will pack the sunscreen.

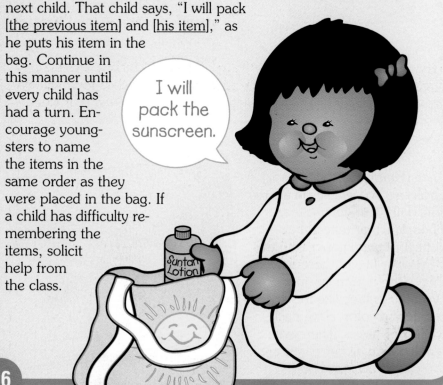

Sea Shapes

Youngsters will dive right into shape recognition when you read *Sea Shapes* by Suse MacDonald (Voyager Picture Books). Before sharing the story, cut a length of blue bulletin board paper to make a mural. From various colors of construction paper, cut a desired number of each shape featured in the story. Give one shape to each child prior to reading. As you turn each page, have youngsters with the matching shape hold it up and name the shape. Then give them ample time to find the shapes in each picture. Afterward, invite each child to paste his shape to the bulletin board paper before using markers to turn it into a sea creature of his own. To embellish the sea creatures and seascape, provide wiggle eyes, sticky dots, and crepe paper streamers. As a finishing touch, use blue watercolor paint to add wavy lines to this ocean so blue.

Out of the Ocean

Sun, sand, and surf—the beach has much to offer. Read *Out of the Ocean* by Debra Frasier (Harcourt Brace & Company) and you'll feel like you're really there! Set up this beach treasure hunt to reinforce the book's message that there are wonderful treasures wherever you look. Gather ocean-related items—such as an assortment of shells, sea glass, seagull feathers, and coral—and hide the items in your outdoor sandbox. (You can find ocean objects at craft stores or aquariums.) Ask each child to bring a beach towel and sunglasses to school. After reading this beautifully illustrated story, grab your beach towels and head for the sun and the sand (the sandbox). Invite a few children at a time to search "the beach" for ocean treasures. Once a treasure is found, have the child bring it back to his towel to examine it. Invite your little beachcombers to exchange treasures. Remind youngsters to remember to look for treasures wherever they go!

Lottie's New Beach Towel

Count on Lottie from *Lottie's New Beach Towel* by Petra Mathers (Atheneum) to inspire your children to dream up lots of new ideas. After reading the book, discuss the clever ways Lottie used her beach towel in the story. Challenge your children to be as ingenious as Lottie. Gather a class supply of scrap materials, each measuring at least six inches square. Give each child one piece and ask her to think of different ways she could use it. Could it be used in a game? Could it be part of a picture? Could it be worn in some way? Give the children enough time to brainstorm; then marvel at their creativity as they share their ingenious ideas with one another.

Swimmy

Are you fishin' for the ideal story to teach your youngsters about the importance of teamwork? Then read aloud *Swimmy* by Leo Lionni (Alfred A. Knopf, Inc.). As an extension, invite your class to work as a team to make a giant fish similar to the one in the story. Set up a painting station with a length of blue bulletin board paper, red and black tempera paint in separate shallow pans, and a black marker. On the paper, lightly pencil in the shape of a giant fish. Ask a child to press one hand into the black paint; then have him hold his fingers together and press his hand onto the fish outline where the eye should be. Have the remaining children make one or more similar handprints—in red—until the fish outline is filled in. Once the paint is dry, invite each child to use the marker to add an eye to her red fish. Add a wiggle eye to further distinguish the black Swimmy. Mount the finished project on a bulletin board to show off your class's terrific teamwork!

Rain

In the Rain With Baby Duck

Have you ever heard of a duck that hates the rain? Well, meet Baby Duck of *In the Rain With Baby Duck* by Amy Hest (Candlewick Press). Baby Duck pouts in the rain, until Grampa comes to the rescue with a bright red umbrella and matching boots. After sharing this delightful story, invite your little ones to make their very own Baby Ducks. To prepare, cut enough small paper plates in half so each child will have one half. Scallop the straight edge of each plate half to resemble an umbrella. For each child, precut a 4-inch circle, a $2\frac{1}{2}$-inch circle, and two 2-inch triangles from yellow construction paper. Also precut a 2-inch diamond from orange construction paper, folding it in half to create a beak shape.

To make Baby Duck, glue a large and small circle to a construction paper background as shown. Glue the beak and two wiggle eyes to the head. Use a red marker to add Baby Duck's boots. To make the umbrella, paint the paper plate half with red paint (or a creative watercolor design). Once the paint is dry, staple a pipe cleaner handle to the umbrella and then glue the umbrella top to the top of the paper. To make Baby Duck look like she is holding the umbrella, glue two yellow triangle wings to the sides of Baby Duck's body and then slide the umbrella "handle" under one of them. Finish the project by using a blue marker to add a little downpour over Baby Duck...who *used to* hate the rain.

Rabbits and Raindrops

Rabbits and Raindrops by Jim Arnosky (The Putnam Publishing Group) is the story of five baby rabbits and their first rain. After sharing this inviting story, encourage your little ones to hold up five fingers and count down with you as you sing the following song.

(sung to the tune of "Five Little Ducks Went Out to Play")

Five baby rabbits went out to play	*Hold up five fingers.*
In the green grass on a sunny day.	*Make a round sun using arms.*
But when the rain began to fall,	*Wiggle fingers downward.*
Under the hedge one rabbit crawled.	*Slide one hand under the other.*
Four baby rabbits...	*Hold up four fingers.*
Three baby rabbits...	*Hold up three fingers.*
Two baby rabbits...	*Hold up two fingers.*
One baby rabbit...	*Hold up one finger.*
No baby rabbits went out to play	*Make a zero with fingers.*
In the green grass on that rainy day.	*Wiggle fingers downward.*
Suddenly the rain did stop,	*Hold palms up and look up.*
So out in the sun five rabbits did hop.	*Hop like rabbits.*

April Showers

"Ladies and gentlemen. Children, too. We've just GOT to do a dance for you." Share *April Showers* by George Shannon (Greenwillow Books) and watch five dancing frogs leap, twirl, and shimmy in the rain. Then do some fancy footwork of your own to the following tune—in rain or shine.

(sung to the tune of "The Hokey-Pokey")

We're gonna [tiptoe-twirl].
We're gonna [tiptoe-twirl].
We're gonna [tiptoe-twirl]
On a rainy, rainy day.
We'll shimmy, shimmy, shimmy,
And we'll turn ourselves around,
All on a rainy day.

Substitute these other dance steps from the story or make up your own:
    step-back-hop
    kick-turn-spin
    dance like fools

Rain

Rain, rain, everywhere! After sharing Robert Kalan's *Rain* (Mulberry Books), let it rain all over your little puddle jumpers as they make their own crayon-resist rain pictures. Gather white paper, crayons, and blue watercolors. Have each child draw a picture of herself wearing a raincoat and boots and carrying an umbrella. (Remind her to push down hard on her crayon while drawing and to color in any shapes she makes.) Have her use a white crayon to add raindrops; then have her paint the entire surface of the paper with watercolors. Who can resist splashin' in the rain?

Mushroom in the Rain

How does one mushroom shelter several animals from the rain? Find out in the Russian tale of *Mushroom in the Rain* (Aladdin Paperbacks) by Mirra Ginsburg. Then invite your youngsters to act out this delightful story. Name six student volunteers as different animals from the story. Have remaining students hold the perimeter of a bedsheet to represent the mushroom. If possible, play a tape recording of rain sounds. As each character approaches the mushroom looking for shelter from the rain, he asks, "Is there room enough for me?" Then the youngsters holding the sheet raise it over their heads to gather air resembling a large mushroom. The first character sits under the mushroom, and then the children lower the sheet to the floor over the character. (For a youngster who may be frightened under the sheet, have another adult sit under the sheet with her.) Continue in this manner, with each additional character joining the others under the mushroom. When the fox asks, "Is there room enough for me?" have the other children say, "No!" and shoo the fox away. Act out the story several times to give all your children a turn to hide under the mushroom in the rain.

The Biggest Boy

Watch big things happen when you read *The Biggest Boy* by Kevin Henkes (Mulberry Books). After sharing the story, talk about the exaggerated things that Billy imagines doing when he grows to be the biggest boy in the world. Ask each child to imagine what he would be able to do if he were the biggest child. Next discuss the things your youngsters are learning to do on their own as they grow bigger, such as getting dressed, answering the telephone, and tying their shoes. Record the "big-kid" things they can do on a chart similar to the one shown.

get dressed alone	answer the phone	brush teeth	tie shoes	feed pets
Casey Elaine Terrell Marcus Kyla	Ruth Casey	A. J. Jonah Kyla	Terrell	Cassi Ruth David Jonah

The Mixed-up Chameleon

Read aloud Eric Carle's *The Mixed-up Chameleon* (HarperTrophy) to teach youngsters that although it is fun to imagine being someone else, being yourself is the only way to be. After sharing the story, invite your little ones to sit in a circle and act out the following song as you sing it to them. Ask youngsters to be just like the chameleon and continue each previous action along with each new action, pretending to have characteristics of all the animals in the song.

(sung to the tune of the Oscar Mayer® weiner theme song)

Oh, I wish I were an eagle in the sky!
That is what I'd truly like to be.
For if I were an eagle in the sky,
I could fly around free as can be.

Flap arms.

Oh, I wish I were a very tall giraffe!
That is what I'd truly like to be.
For if I were a very tall giraffe,
I could reach as high as high can be.

Stretch neck high and flap arms.

Oh, I wish I were a dolphin in the sea!

That is what I'd truly like to be.
For if I were a dolphin in the sea,
I could swim around so gracefully.

Lay on stomach with feet together, stretch neck, and flap arms.

Oh, but I'm really happy being me!
That is who I truly like to be.
I wouldn't want to change from being me,
'Cause I'm a special kid, don't you agree?

Sit up and hug yourself.

Shake head "no."
Point to self; turn palms up and shrug shoulders.

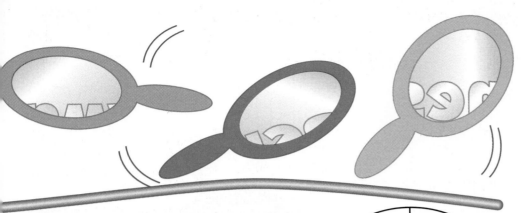

The Little Engine That Could™

After reading aloud the well-loved classic *The Little Engine That Could™* by Watty Piper (Grosset & Dunlap), discuss the powerful words of the Little Blue Engine, "I think I can—I think I can.™" Talk about situations your students have encountered where the "I can" attitude was (or could have been) applied. Then put little ones on the right track to remembering those words with this activity. Seat youngsters in a circle and begin to chant together those same words. Once a rhythm is established, begin tapping your knees as you continue to chant. Next clap your hands to the beat. Finally, have each youngster stand and put his hands on the waist of the child to his right to make a train. Begin marching around the circle to the beat and continue to chant, "I think I can—I think I can." By repeating this positive phrase, the "I can do anything" attitude is bound to stick!

Just Because I Am: A Child's Book of Affirmation

After reading aloud *Just Because I Am: A Child's Book of Affirmation* by Lauren Murphy Payne (Free Spirit Publishing, Inc.), discuss how feelings are something we all share and are a big part of who we are. Then encourage youngsters to share their feelings with the help of these Feelings Wheels. To prepare, draw a nine-inch circle on white paper. Draw lines on the circle to divide it into four sections; then make one photocopy. On each section, write one of these phrases: "I feel anger...," "I feel sadness...," "I feel fear...," or "I feel love..." Under each phrase, draw a face that illustrates that feeling. Photocopy a class supply of both circles; then place them at a center along with brads, crayons, and scissors. Invite children to visit this center to make Feelings Wheels.

To make one, cut out one blank circle and one programmed circle. Use a brad to connect the two circles together in the center, with the programmed wheel on top and the lines matched up. Cut along each line on the top circle, stopping near the brad. Once the lines are cut, lift up one face at a time and draw a picture of a situation related to that feeling on the circle underneath. Then write (or dictate) a description of each feeling near the picture. Encourage youngsters to share their wheels to affirm that we all have similar feelings.

I Like Me!

Help build self-esteem with a reading of *I Like Me!* by Nancy Carlson (Puffin Paperbacks), a story about a self-confident pig who considers herself her best friend. After sharing the story, discuss the importance of liking yourself. Then invite each youngster to reflect upon his own personal best friend with this art activity. Give the child a large sheet of construction paper and a four-inch aluminum foil circle. Instruct him to glue the foil circle to his paper, flattening it out as he presses it down. Then encourage him to draw his body below the foil circle. Write the words "MY BEST FRIEND" outside the top half of his circle to resemble hair. Next encourage the child to hold up his paper and look into the eyes of his best friend...and what a good-looking friend at that!

Shadows

Shadows

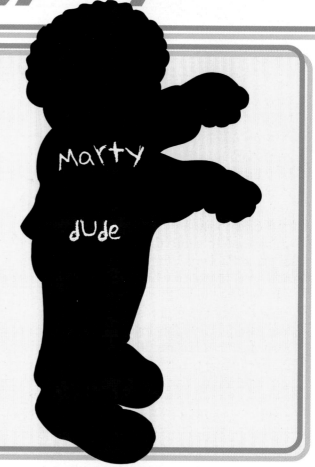

Marty

dUde

I Have a Friend

Who's your constant companion on a sunny day? Your shadow, of course! Read aloud *I Have a Friend* by Keiko Narahashi (Aladdin Paperbacks) and explore the friendship between a boy and his shadow. Then introduce your children to their own shadow friends either by bringing them outdoors on a sunny day or by shining flashlights in a darkened classroom. After youngsters have enjoyed some free play with their shadows, have older youngsters work in pairs to make these shadow projects. Have one child in the pair lie down on a length of black bulletin board paper, striking any pose he desires. Have his partner use chalk to trace around his body. (Trace younger children yourself.) Next, direct each child to cut out his "shadow" and label it with his name and a nickname for his "shadow." When the shadow projects are complete, hang them in your classroom so youngsters can enjoy their shadows in any kind of weather.

This book will *make* a great shadow.

What Makes a Shadow?

Shed some light on the subject of shadows by sharing *What Makes a Shadow?* by Clyde Robert Bulla (HarperCollins Children's Books). As a follow-up, invite your little scientists to experiment with light and dark shadows. To prepare, gather an assortment of items, such as paper towels, construction paper, books, cardboard, tissue paper, clear plastic wrap, and waxed paper. Take the items and your youngsters outside to a bright sunny spot (or use flashlights in a darkened room). Encourage the children to spread out and discover their own shadows. Discuss why their shadows are where they are. Then distribute the items you gathered and invite the children to use them to make more shadows. Which items cast light shadows? Which cast dark shadows? Remind youngsters that the materials that allow some light to shine through (such as tissue paper) make lighter shadows than those that allow no light to shine through (such as books).

Bear Shadow

Getting rid of a shadow is not an easy task, as seen in *Bear Shadow* by Frank Asch (Aladdin Paperbacks). After reading aloud the story, examine together the illustrations on the copyright and dedication pages. Explain why the tree's shadow moved as the day progressed. Then invite youngsters to observe firsthand the movement of shadows. To prepare, photocopy a class supply of the bear pattern (page 62) onto brown construction paper. Encourage each youngster to make a bear puppet by cutting out his bear and gluing it to a craft stick. Then have him insert his puppet into a ball of clay so that it stands alone. At the beginning of a sunny school day, invite your class to bring their bears outdoors. Ask students to find their own space on a blacktop or concrete area. Direct each child to place his puppet on the blacktop and trace its shadow with a piece of chalk. Have youngsters write their names next to their bear outlines and leave their puppets in place; then go indoors. Wait at least one hour; then direct youngsters to return outdoors to their original spots. Leaving their bear puppets in the same place, have youngsters trace the bear shadows again. How does the current shadow compare to the earlier one? Discuss why it moved. How "un-bear-ably" interesting!

Nothing Sticks Like a Shadow

Laughter is sure to stick around long after a reading of Ann Tompert's *Nothing Sticks Like a Shadow* (Houghton Mifflin Company). Rabbit tries to run from, hide from, sweep away, and snip off his shadow, but he is unsuccessful. After reading the story, see if youngsters can be more successful at ridding themselves of their shadows. Gather some scissors and a few brooms; then bring the items and the class outdoors on a sunny day. Remind them of these things Rabbit did to escape his shadow: running from it, hiding behind a tree or bush, sweeping it away with a broom, pulling it apart from him, and snipping it away with scissors. Then challenge youngsters to try Rabbit's tactics for shadow removal or invent some strategies of their own. Is it true? Does nothing stick like a shadow?

Shadows and Reflections

Shadow? Or reflection? After this sharing of Tana Hoban's magnificent photographs in *Shadows and Reflections* (Greenwillow Books), youngsters will know the difference between the two—without a shadow of a doubt! Prior to sharing the book, give each child a crayon and a sheet of paper with the letter *S* (for shadows) written in one column and the letter *R* (for reflection) written in the other. Explain to youngsters that you are about to share a book of photographs that show both *shadows* and *reflections*. Talk about the definition of each term and show examples. As you share each photograph in the book, have students decide whether they see a shadow or a reflection and then mark the appropriate column on their papers with a tally mark. At the end of the book, have them count their tally marks to see if there were more examples of shadows or reflections. Then confirm their results by revisiting the book and identifying each picture together.

For further exploration, invite your little ones to make some shadows and reflections of their own. Gather these items for making reflections: a large flat container of water, a mirror, a large aluminum pot lid, and a length of aluminum foil. Gather other items that might cast interesting shadows. Bring your class and the gathered items outdoors on a sunny day. Place the items on the ground and invite youngsters to make shadows or reflections using the objects. Provide assistance only if needed—discovery learning is fun!

Millions of Snowflakes

Count on Mary McKenna Siddals' *Millions of Snowflakes* (Clarion Books) to warm up even the coldest day. This playful counting poem progresses from one snowflake to millions of gently falling snowflakes. For a frosty followup, set up a snowflake center with white tempera paint, iridescent glitter, a shallow box, and wagon wheel pasta (or thread spools). Fold large sheets of blue or lavender construction paper in half. On one half of each folded sheet of paper, write the numerals 1 to 5 in a column. On the other half, write "Millions of Snowflakes."

At this center, a child dips the pasta (or spool) into the paint and then stamps the corresponding number of snowflakes beside each numeral. On the side labeled "Millions of Snowflakes," the child stamps snowflakes to her heart's content. Then she places her paper inside the box and sprinkles the wet snowflakes with iridescent glitter. You'll see millions of sparkling snowflakes falling everywhere!

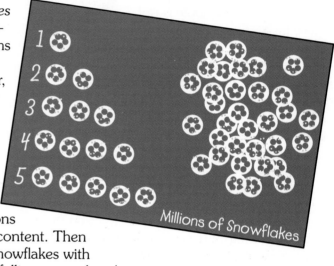

Millions of Snowflakes

The Snowy Day

Delight in the wonders of the deep, deep snow with a reading of Ezra Jack Keats' *The Snowy Day* (Viking Press). This Caldecott Medal winner is an absolute "must read" after a fresh snowfall. After sharing this snowy tale, invite your little ones to try this snowy science experiment. Bring in buckets of snow to fill your water table (or fill the table with crushed ice). Make a snowball and place it in a resealable plastic bag. Then put the bag inside a coat pocket. Hang the coat where youngsters can reach it, so that they can pull the snowball from the pocket to see whether it melts as Peter's did in the story. While the children are waiting for the snowball to disappear, invite them to enjoy the frosty fun in the water table.

Snowballs

What can you do with a snowball? Make snowfolks, of course! Lois Ehlert's *Snowballs* (Harcourt Brace & Company) is chock-full of snow people and snow animals made with a little help from some "good stuff in a sack." If there is snow where you live, gather your own "good stuff" and take it outdoors on a snowy day to decorate snow figures that your youngsters make in the snow. Then, if you're hungry from all that snowperson building, follow the recipe at the end of the book for making popcorn balls. Or make these yummy snowfolk faces. Gather a class supply of popcorn (or rice) cakes, white cream cheese (or frosting), and small bowls of edible "good stuff," such as raisins, M&Ms® candies, pretzels, or popped popcorn. Invite each child to spread cream cheese on his popcorn cake and then use the other items to make an original snow person or snow animal face.

Elmer in the Snow

David McKee's *Elmer in the Snow* (Lothrop, Lee & Shepard Books) is sure to be a big hit as your youngsters watch Elmer introduce his elephant friends to their first snow experience. If your youngsters are unfamiliar with Elmer, be sure to share David McKee's other Elmer adventures with the class. Then follow up with this elephant extension. Set up your art table with colored and white construction paper, glue, scissors, markers, salt, and paintbrushes. Make a mixture of half salt and half water. Use the pattern on page 63 to cut several Elmer patterns from tagboard.

At this center, a child traces and then cuts two Elmer patterns from white construction paper. He paints one elephant with the salt mixture to make a frozen Elmer. While his painting is drying, he uses a light-colored marker to make vertical and horizontal lines on his other elephant cutout. Then he uses markers to color in the squares to resemble the patchwork Elmer. Finally, he folds a sheet of colored paper in half and glues one Elmer to each half. "Weather" in the snow or sun, Elmer is always lots of fun!

Rainsong/Snowsong

Rainsong/Snowsong by Philemon Sturges (North-South Books Inc.) is a joyful celebration of a summer's rain and a winter's snow in delightful rhyming text. This book, with its irresistible illustrations, provides the perfect opportunity to discuss rainwear and snow gear. After reading the story, revisit the illustrations, calling youngsters' attention to the clothing. Then gather these clothes from the rainsong: a rain slicker, a pair of boots, and a rain hat (or umbrella). Collect these clothes from the snowsong: a scarf, a pair of mittens, and a snow hat. Put the clothing in your dramatic-play area and encourage youngsters to sort the clothing into a rainsong stack and a snowsong stack. Then invite them to try on the clothes and pretend to frolic in the rain and snow.

Space

Mooncake

Cook up some fun with a reading of *Mooncake* by Frank Asch (Aladdin Paperbacks). Then follow up with your own recipe for moon-cake. In advance, combine in a blender (or with a mixer) one quart of vanilla ice cream and a 12-ounce can of frozen lemonade. Blend the mixture until it is soft; then scoop it into a round cake pan and freeze it. After reading the book aloud to your class, invite them to climb into their rocket ships (under desks or tables) and prepare for a journey to the Moon. Begin a countdown, but have them pretend to fall asleep before reaching the number 1, just as Bear did in the story. When they "awaken," they will find themselves on the Moon! They're sure to be hungry from their trip, so give each space traveler a plastic spoon and a cup. Invite each child to use an ice-cream scoop to serve herself some mooncake. Mmmmm...out of this world!

Note: This recipe makes enough for 15–20 single scoops.

Zoom! Zoom! Zoom! I'm Off to the Moon!

Read *Zoom! Zoom! Zoom! I'm Off to the Moon!* by Dan Yaccarino (Scholastic Trade Books) and take rhyming to the outer limits! Take advantage of the rollicking rhymes in this story to build language skills. As you read the story aloud a second time, invite the children to complete selected rhymes from the book, such as these:

Zoom! Zoom! Zoom! I'm off to the ___. *(Moon)*
Up, up, and away, I'm leaving ____. *(today)*
There's outer space all over the ____. *(place)*
Floating around without a _____. *(sound)*

Then challenge youngsters further by providing only one rhyming word from the text and asking students to provide the word that rhymes with it, such as *space* and *place*. Watch those rhyming skills rocket sky-high!

Floating around without a...

sound !

Me and My Place in Space

Blast off your unit on space with a reading of *Me and My Place in Space* by Joan Sweeney (Dragonfly Books). After reading the story, discuss how all the planets—including Earth—circle around the Sun. To illustrate this concept, have each youngster cut out a yellow construction paper circle and glue it to the center of a sheet of black paper. Then place the black paper inside a box lid. Drop a marble dipped in fluorescent paint inside the lid, and then move the box in a circular motion to make the marble planet rotate around its paper sun. It's "sun-sational!"

Shoot for the stars with a reading of *I Want to Be an Astronaut* by Byron Barton (HarperCollins Children's Books). After sharing the story, return to the pages that show the astronauts floating in space and explain the term *zero gravity*. Then demonstrate the concept with this gravity game. Ask the children to form a circle around you in an open space. Blow up a balloon and explain that they are all on a team playing against *gravity*—the force that is pulling the balloon down to Earth. The object of the game is to try to keep the balloon up in the air to defeat the force of gravity. If the balloon touches the ground, gravity scores a point. If the team keeps the balloon in the air for a count of three, the team scores a point. May the force be with you!

Grandpa Takes Me to the Moon

After sharing the story *Grandpa Takes Me to the Moon* by Timothy R. Gaffney (William Morrow and Company, Inc.), ignite your youngsters' imaginations by pretending the sand in your sand table is the surface of the Moon. Use a spray bottle of water to moisten the sand. Put LEGO® (or DUPLO®) blocks and toy people near the sand table, along with some pebbles, a potato masher, and a small American flag. Have the children use the potato masher to make craters on the Moon's surface. Scatter the Moon rocks (pebbles). Encourage youngsters to use the blocks to make a Moon lander and a lunar rover. Provide Gaffney's book as a reference. Before returning to Earth, have your little astronauts leave their mark by planting the American flag on the Moon.

Spiders and Bats

Spider on the Floor

Spin together some hilarious fun as you read *Spider on the Floor* by Bill Russell (Crown Publishers, Inc.). If desired, play Raffi's song "Spider on the Floor," on the album *Singable Songs for the Very Young* (Troubadour Records Ltd.), as you display the pages of the book. Then continue the fun by making spider finger puppets. To make one, glue together two black pom-poms of different sizes for the spider's body. Squeeze glue onto the center of a ³⁄₄" x 2" tagboard strip; then drape four 3-inch lengths of black yarn over the glue (as shown). Glue the spider body over the yarn pieces so that there are four yarn legs on each side of the body. When the glue is dry, help the child wrap the tagboard strip around the tip of his index finger; then secure it with tape. During a second reading of the story, invite youngsters to move their finger puppets to the different body parts mentioned in the book.

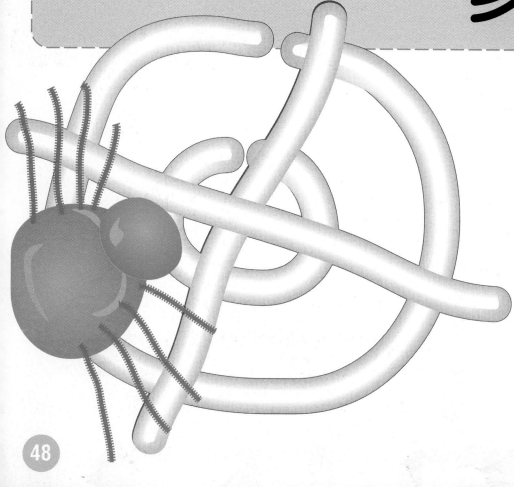

The Very Busy Spider

Get busy reading *The Very Busy Spider* by Eric Carle (The Putnam Publishing Group). Then invite your youngsters to illustrate this popular story using clay. Set up a center with red, green, and white clay (or soft play dough for younger children) and pipe cleaners that have been cut in half. Encourage each student to use her imagination as she works with the clay to form a spider's body and head. Invite her to count eight pipe cleaner halves to use as spider legs. Then show her how to roll thin clay ropes to make a spiderweb. Encourage youngsters to feel the final product just as they can feel Carle's webs in the story.

Stellaluna

Youngsters are sure to go batty over a reading of *Stellaluna* by Janell Cannon (Voyager Picture Books). As a fun follow-up, invite each youngster to make his own Stellaluna. First fold a sheet of brown construction paper in half. Have the child place his thumb on the fold and spread his fingers just a bit. Then trace around his hand. With the paper still folded, have him cut out his handprint and then open it to reveal a one-of-a-kind bat shape. Encourage him to cut bat feet from the paper scraps and glue them to his bat. As a finishing touch, have him stick on two white paper reinforcers for eyes. If desired, hang the bats upside down from a clothesline (or string) in your classroom.

The Itsy Bitsy Spider

Read or sing along to Iza Trapani's extended version of *The Itsy Bitsy Spider* (Whispering Coyote Press, Inc.). After enjoying Trapani's delightful illustrations and additional verses to this ever-popular song, invite your little spider lovers to use watercolors (as Trapani did) to illustrate a page from the story. To prepare, write the verse shown at the bottom of a sheet of white copy paper. Photocopy a class supply; then distribute the papers to your class. Discuss things the children may wish to include in their illustrations, such as a tree, the spider, the sun, and a self-portrait. If desired, make your own watercolor illustration to use as an example.

Encourage little ones to use pencil to draw simple outlines before filling in each outline with watercolors. When the illustrations are complete, display them with the title "The Itsy Bitsy Spider and Me!"

The itsy bitsy spider climbed up the maple tree.
She slipped on some dew and landed next to me.

Bat Jamboree

It will be standing room only during your reading of Kathi Appelt's *Bat Jamboree* (Mulberry Books). As a follow-up to this sassy, rhythmic counting book, have your little bat lovers sing the following song with "bat-itude."

(sung to the tune of "Sing a Song of Sixpence")

At the bat jamboree
The bats put on a show.
See them build a pyramid
Standing in ten rows.
1, 2, 3, 4, 5, 6,
7, 8, 9, 10.
Until the bat lady sings
You know the fun won't end!

Flap like a bat.

Put thumbs and fingertips together to form triangle.
Hold up ten fingers.
Count six fingers.
Count remaining fingers.
Sing, "Laa."

49

Thanksgiving

The Tasty Thanksgiving Feast: A Lift-the-Flap Book

The Tasty Thanksgiving Feast: A Lift-the-Flap Book by Suzy-Jane Tanner (HarperCollins Publishers, Inc.) is sure to satisfy your youngsters' appetites for a good story. Discuss how each of Henrietta's friends contributed something to their Thanksgiving feast. Then follow up your reading with this critical-thinking activity. To prepare, gather several Thanksgiving feast-related items, such as a fork or spoon, a can of cranberry sauce, a can of pumpkin pie filling, a magazine picture of a roasted turkey, an empty box of stuffing mix, a squash, and an ear of corn. Place the items in a paper grocery bag. Place one item in a basket and cover the top of the basket with a festive cloth napkin. After sharing Tanner's story, show youngsters the basket and give them clues to help them guess what's under the napkin. After youngsters have had a chance to guess, have a child reveal it for the class. Continue this guessing game with the other items in the bag.

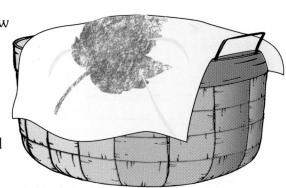

Dear Class,

Today is our annual Thanksgiving feast. Patsy Pig has given me so many jobs that I just can't find the time to make pumpkin pizza pies this year. Could you please make your own to bring to the feast? Thanks so much for your help.

Albert

P.S. I have sent the crusts to help you get started.

Albert's Thanksgiving

Every time Albert tries to harvest the vegetables for the Thanksgiving feast, Patsy Pig sends a message requesting his help for something else! Will the vegetables ever be ready for the feast? Find out by reading *Albert's Thanksgiving* by Leslie Tryon (Aladdin Paperbacks). After sharing the story with the class, have an adult come to the door delivering a note (like the one shown) and a class supply of large, round sugar cookies. Read the note to the class. Then take out a tray of these ingredients: sweetened pumpkin pie filling, whipped cream, and chocolate chips (or raisins). Invite youngsters to spread the sweetened pumpkin pie filling on their cookies (pizza crusts), spoon on some whipped cream, and top off the pizzas with chocolate chips. Once the pizzas are done, pretend it's time for the feast and dig in!

Thanksgiving Treat

The smallest member of the family feels left out of the Thanksgiving preparations, until Grandpa steps in and suggests they gather chestnuts together in *Thanksgiving Treat* by Catherine Stock (Aladdin Paperbacks). Gather (or purchase) some chestnuts of your own to share with the class. Cut a few chestnuts open, and invite youngsters to observe the meat inside. If possible, show the children a *bur*—the prickly seed case that chestnuts develop in. If a real bur is not available, show little ones the illustration of a bur on the book's title page. Then follow up by taking your class outdoors to search for other nuts or seeds that may have fallen from autumn trees. Encourage youngsters to place nuts and other interesting nature items they collect in your science center for all to observe.

Gracias, the Thanksgiving Turkey

Miguel's father sends him a turkey with instructions to fatten the bird up for Thanksgiving, but Miguel has a different plan in mind for his fine-feathered friend. Read *Gracias, the Thanksgiving Turkey* by Joy Cowley (Scholastic Trade Books) to find out what happens to this lovable turkey. Then give older students a little lesson in Spanish using the Spanish words from the book. Before reading the story, copy the Spanish words listed in the book's glossary onto a sheet of chart paper. (Do not record the English translations yet.) Share the cover and title of the book with the children, and then ask them if they know what the word *gracias* means. Explain that the story features Spanish words that they will learn later. After reading the story once to enjoy the plot, reread the story and encourage youngsters to raise their hands *every* time they hear a word that sounds Spanish. Encourage the class to use context clues to decipher the meaning of each Spanish word they hear. Then record the English translation on the chart paper. If desired, have the class dictate a note for Miguel's father asking him to spare Gracias's life. Wherever possible, substitute Spanish words from your list in the class note.

Abuela	grandmother
Abuelo	grandfather
amiga	friend (girl)
amigos	friends
Gracias	thank you
hijo	son
loco	crazy

A Turkey for Thanksgiving

Turkey is the guest of honor, not the main course, in *A Turkey for Thanksgiving* by Eve Bunting (Clarion Books). Extend youngsters' enjoyment of this story with a turkey hunt of your own. In advance, make a brown construction paper headband with craft feathers glued to the back. Seat the children in a circle; then ask one student volunteer to close his eyes (or wear a blindfold) while you quietly send another volunteer off to a hidden area of the room wearing the headband. When the turkey is safely hidden, ask the first volunteer to open his eyes and look at the circle of children to determine the identity of the hidden turkey. Once he has figured it out, have him retrieve the turkey from her hiding place and invite her to Thanksgiving dinner (back to the circle). Repeat the game until all your little turkeys have had a chance to participate.

Transportation

Freight Train

All aboard! Start your transportation unit off on the right track with Donald Crews' *Freight Train* (Mulberry Books). After enjoying this colorful book of chug-along movement, set up your very own train-making station with DUPLO® or LEGO® blocks and varied lengths of colorful yarn. Demonstrate for your little engineers how to use the yarn to connect the blocks together like a train. Lay one end of a length of yarn between two stacked blocks; then snap the blocks together to secure the yarn. Continue to snap pairs of blocks together with the yarn in between until you have your very own train to chug along on the floor. After practicing this train-making technique, encourage youngsters to look in the story for other objects to build with the blocks, such as tunnels and trestles. Full steam ahead!

Wheels on the Bus

Sing merrily along to the familiar text of *Wheels on the Bus,* a Raffi Songs to Read™ book (Crown Publishers, Inc.). While this humorous book deals with city transportation, your children may be more familiar with a school bus. So encourage them to sing these additional verses about how to be safe and polite on a school bus.

The wheels on the bus go round and round,
Round and round, round and round.
The wheels on the bus go round and round,
On the way to school.

The children on the bus stay in their seats....
The children on the bus talk quietly....
The children on the bus exit in a line....
The children on the bus thank the bus driver....

Let's Fly From A to Z

Watch skills take off after a reading of Doug Magee and Robert Newman's *Let's Fly From A to Z* (Cobblehill Books). Use this alphabet book about airplanes to reinforce letter skills. For younger students, give each child a die-cut letter and ask him to hold it up when you read about an aircraft item that begins with his letter. For older students, use the book as motivation to create a transportation alphabet book. Write the letters of the alphabet in a column on a sheet of chart paper. Brainstorm together transportation words that begin with each letter. (Encourage the children to refer to classroom transportation books for help.) Once the list is complete, ask youngsters to illustrate the words from your list, making a separate page for each word. Add text to each illustration, such as "A is for airplane." Bind the pages in alphabetical order between construction paper covers and add the title "The ABCs of Transportation." Don't be surprised to find a traffic jam at your reading center!

C is for canoe.

Fire Engines

Anne Rockwell's *Fire Engines* (Puffin Books) describes all the modes of transportation that firefighters use. After sharing the book, teach children the following countdown fingerplay about firefighters and their vehicles. Encourage youngsters to hold up the corresponding number of fingers to represent the firefighters. As you recite the rhyme together, show the pages from the story that feature the named vehicles.

Five firefighters, ready every day.
To the ladder truck! There's a call today!
Four firefighters, ready every day.
To the pumper truck! There's a call today!
Three firefighters, ready every day.
To the ambulance! There's a call today!
Two firefighters, ready every day.
To the fireboat! There's a call today!
One firefighter, ready every day.
He's the chief, and he leads the way!

Boats Afloat

A reading of *Boats Afloat* by Shelley Rotner (Orchard Books) will chart the course for a boat-building center. In advance, ask youngsters to bring to school items that float, such as foam meat trays, milk cartons, margarine tubs, bars of Ivory® soap, sponges, and wood scraps. Set up a center with toothpicks, craft sticks, craft foam, glue, and the items brought from home. Then invite youngsters to create their own unique ship designs using the materials provided. Encourage the children to refer to the book to help them decide which types of boats to build. Provide rocks for barges, netting for fishing boats, toy airplanes and helicopters for aircraft carriers, and toy people for ferries. Once youngsters have completed their ships, have them test the waters at your water table to see if their boats are truly shipshape. Bon voyage!

Valentine's Day

Froggy's First Kiss

When Froggy receives an unexpected display of affection, his heart plays leapfrog in Jonathan London's *Froggy's First Kiss* (Viking Children's Books). After sharing this sweet story, invite each youngster to make a Froggy or a Frogilina from heart shapes. To prepare, cut two heart-shaped patterns from tagboard, making one tall and thin and the other short and wide. Cut a pair of large ovals from white construction paper for each child. Also cut lengths of orange and yellow curling ribbon and a supply of construction paper hair bows.

To make a frog, trace the heart shapes onto a 12" x 18" sheet of green construction paper; then cut them out. Glue the short, wide heart to the bottom half of the tall, thin heart to make the frog's face. Glue the white oval eyes to the top of the face. Use a black crayon to draw pupils and a big grin. To turn the frog into Frogilina, tape several pieces of curling ribbon to the back side of the frog's head; then curl them with scissors to create curls. Glue a decorated construction paper bow to the top of the frog's head. To finish off each Froggy, invite the child to put on some red lipstick before planting a big juicy kiss on Froggy's face!

Arthur's Valentine

Your little cupids will be tickled pink to discover Arthur's secret admirer in *Arthur's Valentine* by Marc Brown (Little, Brown and Company). After reading the story, invite youngsters to play this guessing game involving their own secret admirers. To prepare, draw a heart on a sheet of paper; then write this message on the heart: "Your secret admirer is wearing _____." Photocopy a class supply of the heart onto red construction paper. Have each child cut out a heart; then help him fill in the blank with a brief description of what he is wearing. Encourage him to decorate the heart with valentine stickers; then help him tape a candy kiss to the heart. Once all the hearts are complete, place them in a valentine gift bag. Invite one child at a time to select a heart from the bag; then say the following poem together. Read the message on the heart and ask the child to guess the identity of his secret admirer.

Your secret admirer is wearing _a blue sweater._

Apples, bananas, peaches, a pear,
Can you guess who I am
By the clothes that I wear?

Heart to Heart

In *Heart to Heart* by George Shannon (Houghton Mifflin Company), Squirrel gives Mole a valentine made with memorabilia from special times they spent together. Invite your youngsters to collect memorabilia from a special day spent with friends. Divide the class into pairs. Encourage each pair of valentine pals to stay together throughout the day. Give them a large resealable plastic bag with their names on it. Encourage them to collect a token from each activity they engage in together, such as a small block, an art material, a puzzle piece, a book, or a dress-up item. At the end of the day, have each set of valentine pals share the contents of their bag with the class and recall the fun they had together.

Franklin's Valentines

Touch your youngsters' hearts with a reading of *Franklin's Valentines* by Paulette Bourgeois and Sharon Jennings (Cartwheel Books). Franklin and his classmates celebrate the meaning of true friendship at their valentine party. Celebrate in the same way with your little friends, and make these turtle cupcakes as a delicious party treat. In advance, prepare the following for each child: one mini cupcake, a tablespoon of white frosting tinted with green food coloring, a green Gummy Worm® cut into four 1-inch pieces, one green gumdrop, and one half of a walnut shell (with the nut removed). Place the items on a paper plate, along with a craft stick.

After reading the story to the class, discuss how Franklin learned from his friends a lesson in giving. Then invite each child to make a Franklin cupcake to give to a friend. Have her use a craft stick to spread the frosting onto her cupcake. Have her place the walnut shell half on the frosted cupcake to resemble Franklin's shell. Next have her add a gumdrop head and Gummy Worm arms and legs. Encourage your little ones to exchange cupcakes in the name of friendship. (Be sure youngsters remove the walnut shell halves before munching their party treats!)

It's Nice to Share Valentine's Day with Someone You Love

The Valentine Bears

Eve Bunting's *The Valentine Bears* (Clarion Books) is a story that "bears" rereading! As a fun follow-up, invite youngsters to make a sign like the lovely one Mrs. Bear made for Mr. Bear. Write "It's Nice to Share Valentine's Day With Someone You Love" inside a heart-shaped outline. Make a photocopy on red construction paper for each child. Have each child cut out a heart and glue it to a sheet of 12" x 18" white construction paper. Provide valentine art supplies, such as heart-shaped stickers and stamps, red and white yarn, red and silver glitter, and paper doilies. Encourage each youngster to put her heart into decorating her sign. When the finishing touches are complete, have her roll it up and tie it with red curling ribbon to take home to her loved ones.

GOOD NIGHT, GORILLA

Good Night, Gorilla by Peggy Rathmann (The Putnam Publishing Group) is sure to get your group gigglin' as they watch Gorilla and his friends follow the zookeeper home for an uninvited sleepover! Keep the giggles going with this fun extension. To prepare, duplicate several copies of the small animal patterns on page 64; then cut them apart. Gather the following items for each child: an individual-serving-size cereal box, a 6" x 9" piece of construction paper, a 4" x 4" square of fabric, a school photo, and a 9" x 12" sheet of construction paper.

To make a miniature bed, a child wraps his cereal box in the 6" x 9" construction paper, securing the paper with tape. Next he chooses a zoo animal cutout and trims around the animal's head. He also trims around his head in his school photo. Then he glues them next to each other as shown. He glues a fabric square to the box to resemble a bed cover. Then he glues the bed to the 9" x 12" sheet of construction paper. Help each child finish his project by programming his sheet similarly to the one shown. Display these bedtime scenes on a bulletin board with the title "Good Night, Zoo!"

Charles would like to have a sleepover with a monkey.

ZOO-LOOKING

Enjoy a trip to the zoo as you read *Zoo-Looking* by Mem Fox (Mondo Publishing). After a first reading, share the story again and encourage youngsters to join you as you read the repetitive text. Next invite your little ones to go "zoo-looking" right in their classroom. To prepare for this activity, enlarge the large animal patterns on page 64 and duplicate them onto tagboard. Color them, and then cut around each animal's head. Tape a craft stick to each one. Give the resulting animal masks to selected youngsters and ask them to stand in different areas of your classroom. Invite other children to take turns role-playing zoo visitors. As a child walks by each animal, ask the class to recite this line from the book: "[Child's name] looked at the [animal's name] and the [animal's name] looked back." Encourage each child holding a mask to make movements or sounds that represent his animal. Continue until every youngster has had a turn to role-play a zoo animal or a zoo visitor.

He was too hungry!
I sent him back.

GOING TO THE ZOO

You can bet youngsters will tune right into Tom Paxton's *Going to the Zoo* (William Morrow and Company, Inc.). After introducing each animal in the story, invite your little ones to sing the familiar chorus. Since youngsters will be roarin' for more, continue this zany day at the zoo by listening to the musical version on Paxton's album *Goin' to the Zoo* (Rounder Records). Divide the class into groups of animals that are featured in the song. As you play the song, watch your little monkeys scritch, scritch, scratchin' and your little seals clap, clap, clappin' along to the music. All your little zoo animals are sure to go wild with delight!

DEAR ZOO

After several failed attempts to respond to a child's request for a pet, the zoo finally sends just the right animal in *Dear Zoo* by Rod Campbell (Little Simon). During a second reading of this story, use a sheet of paper to cover each zoo animal. Read the text, omitting the name of the animal. Encourage youngsters to listen for clues in the text. Then challenge them to guess the name of the animal.

To follow up, make a class version of the story. For each child, cut out a tagboard shipping crate—like the one shown in the story. Provide animal magazines or copies of the large animal patterns on page 64. Have each child cut out a zoo animal and glue it to a sheet of construction paper. Then staple the tagboard crate over the animal so that the crate can be lifted to reveal the animal. Record the child's description of why he had to send the animal back to the zoo. As you read the completed book aloud, invite the class to guess the zoo animal hidden in (under) each crate.

SAM WHO NEVER FORGETS

Just when Elephant thinks he has been forgotten, Sam the zookeeper comes along with a feast fit for an elephant in Eve Rice's *Sam Who Never Forgets* (William Morrow and Company, Inc.). After reading the book, put your little zookeepers to work feeding the zoo animals. To prepare for this activity, cut from construction paper 11 each of leaves, bananas, fish, and berries. Gather a wagon and these suggested stuffed animals: a giraffe, a monkey, a seal, and a bear. (Other stuffed animals and corresponding construction paper foods can be substituted.) Place the animals in different areas of your classroom. Next, label each of four containers with a different numeral from 1 to 10. Tape a different construction paper food to each container; then put the containers and food in the wagon.

Invite a child to be the zookeeper. Have him count the corresponding number of zoo foods into the containers and then deliver the food to the appropriate zoo animals. (If needed, have him refer to the book to see which foods to give to each animal.) Remind him not to forget anyone!

Rabbit Pattern
Use with *Rabbit's Good News* on page 4.

Shoes Pattern
Use with *The Country Bunny and the Little Gold Shoes* on page 5.

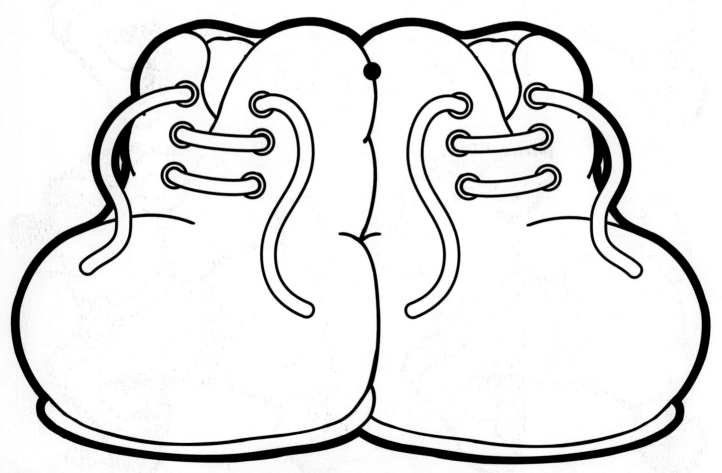

Animal Patterns

Use with *The Little Red Hen* on page 15.

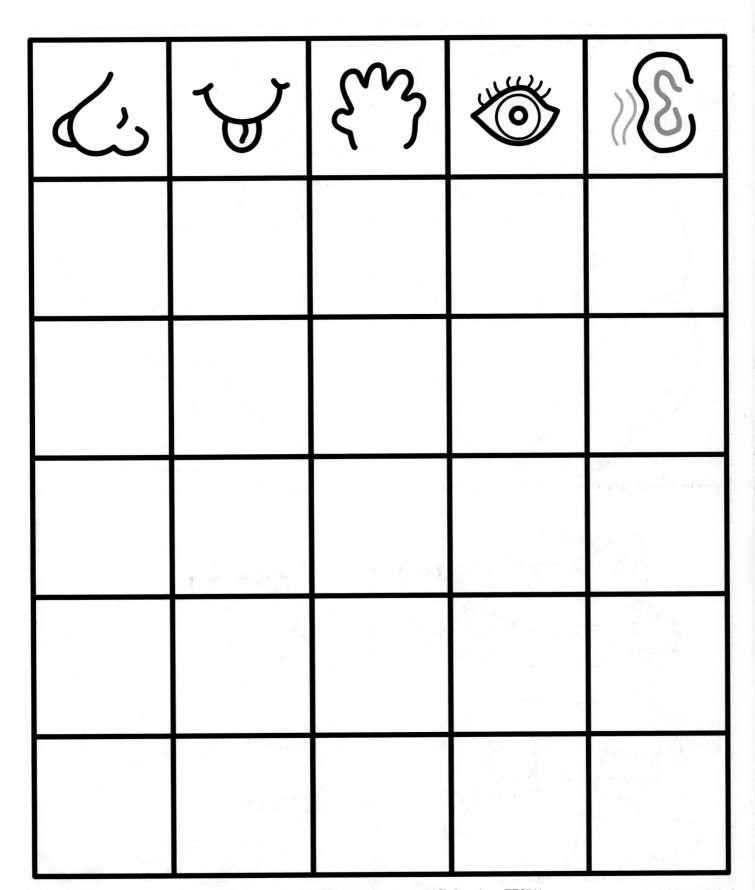

Note to the teacher: Use with "Another 'Sense-ational' Idea" on page 23.

Booklet Text
Use with *Jack's Garden* on page 27.

1. **This is the garden our class planted.**

2. **This is the soil that made up the garden our class planted.**

3. **These are the seeds that we planted in the soil that made up the garden our class planted.**

4. **This is the rain that watered the seeds that we planted in the soil that made up the garden our class planted.**

5. **And these are the plants that grew after the rain that watered the seeds that we planted in the soil that made up the garden our class planted.**

Bear Pattern
Use with *Bear Shadow* on page 43.

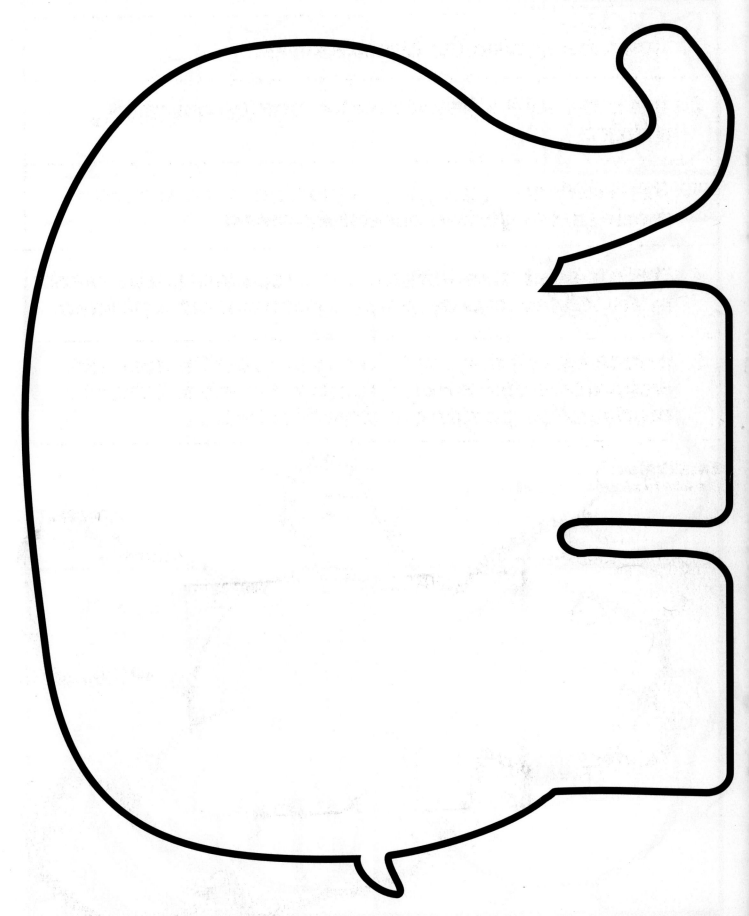

Small Animal Patterns

Use with *Good Night, Gorilla* on page 56.

Large Animal Patterns

Use with *Zoo-Looking* on page 56 and *Dear Zoo* on page 57.